This book is lovingly dedicated to my wife,
Pearlie H. Taylor, whose devotion
was instrumental in my completing the text.

Contents

Illustrations and Tables

Foreword

Informal assessment of individuals with disabilities has undergone major revisions in recent years due chiefly to federal, state, and local laws and mandates. Historically, the major assessment component dealt with assessing individuals using standardized methods. It was soon recognized that other human functions not measured by standardized methods should be assessed to provide a complete picture of strengths and weaknesses of individuals with disabilities. The author of this textbook is taking cognizance not only of the impact of federal, state, and local mandates but also emergent philosophical approaches to educating these individuals, which should be based upon comprehensive assessment of all traits.

Taylor realizes that informal assessments must be *integrated* and infused into the instructional program, as well as used to *identify* related services, *categorize* areas of disabilities, *formulate* the Individualized Education Plan, and *make* appropriate placement decisions. The author explains these procedures in great detail throughout the textbook.

Informal assessment is at the heart of classroom instruction. Data from these assessments can assist educators in understanding the various learning styles of children and in developing functional curricula. The major purpose of this book is to explain how to interpret and use information to plan instruction that will promote the learning of children.

Rose Dutton-Sells, Ph.D.
Core Faculty
The Union Institute and University

Preface

This book is written principally for prospective and in-service teachers who desire to know how using informal assessment techniques can enhance planning for and meeting the individual needs of children.

Assessment skills outlined in the text include a variety of techniques that can support standardized test results. Practical applications of the techniques are articulated for teachers' use.

Information contained in this text was derived from a variety of sources, but mainly from interacting with and observing teachers and children at the Rosemont Elementary School in Baltimore, Maryland.

Acknowledgments

This book is written for all stakeholders responsible for assessing children. The text is premised upon the notion that informal assessment techniques should assist all stakeholders in making appropriate educational decisions in instructing children.

Many individuals have contributed to the final revision of this text. I would like to acknowledge Drs. Geraldine R. Waters and Thomas E. Terrell for reviewing the manuscript and making pointed suggestions for improvement. I thank the editorial staff at Scarecrow Education Press for their assistance, for without it this text could not have been published. A special thank you is extended to Mrs. Emma Crosby for her commitment and dedication in typing and retyping numerous drafts of the manuscript.

CHAPTER 1

Informal Assessment Strategies for Teachers

Classroom teachers should assume the responsibility for assessing the strengths and weaknesses of students in their classrooms through the use of informal assessment techniques. The use of formal techniques can also yield valuable assessment information (see Taylor 2002). The author has elected to emphasize informal assessment techniques. The teacher has more control over the types of informal assessment techniques to employ. These techniques may be designed to assess prior knowledge, to determine skills that students may have mastered, and to monitor progress, provide feedback, make judgments, and grade students' progress and achievement in curriculum areas (Arends 2000).

According to Popham (2002), "Assessment is a broad and relatively non-restrictive label for the kinds of testing and measuring that teachers must do. It is a label to help remind educators that the measurement of students' status should include more than paper and pencil instruments. Assessment is a word that embraces diverse kinds of tests and measurements" (p. 5).

DIAGNOSING PRIOR KNOWLEDGE

Assessing prior knowledge is important for several reasons. First, the teacher needs to be aware of what the student is bringing to the learning environment. Second, information is needed to plan appropriately for intervention strategies to remediate deficits and provide students with feedback on how well they are progressing in selected academic subjects. Third, assessment data should pinpoint the types of human and physical resources needed to support the intervention strategies. Fourth, assessment should determine whether students are moving satisfactorily toward instructional outcomes. Fifth, a variety of assessment techniques should be employed in assessing prior knowledge such as observations, posing probing questions, and interviews. These techniques are discussed at length in chapters 2 and 11. Sixth, diagnosing prior knowledge will enable the classroom teacher to determine the types of examinations to give students, as well as the sequence for reporting grades to parents. Teachers need to be apprised of the aforementioned informal assessment devices, as well as how to construct them and how to judge the effectiveness of them.

DESIGNING AN INFORMATION ASSESSMENT SYSTEM

Information assessment techniques denote that teachers plan their own techniques for diagnosing and analyzing assessment data. The various types of information assessment strategies are detailed in chapters 3 and 11. This section is designed to discuss some principles advocated by Gronlund (1991, 1998) in developing an assessment system.

1. Assess All Instructional Objectives. The teacher should test students on the learning objectives covered in the instructional process. Test items not germane to the instructional objectives should not be included.
2. An Assessment System and Testing Should Cover All Cognitive Domains. Test items should be written on all cognitive levels, including recall of factual information, application, analysis, critical thinking skills, and making evaluative judgments on information (Bloom 1956).
3. Use a Variety of Testing Formats. Develop test items to measure certain abilities. To measure recall, the teacher may want to use matching, true or false, or completion test items; essay and multiple-choice items may be used to measure high-order thinking skills. The age, abilities, and disabilities of the children should also be taken into consideration when using a test format. Teachers should select the type of testing format that best fits the characteristics of the pupils.
4. Make Tests as Valid and Reliable as Possible. Teachers should strive to make tests as valid and reliable as possible. Procedures for conducting validity and reliability are beyond the scope of this

text; refer to any basic book on assessment. However, the larger the number of test items the more reliable the test tends to be. Clearly written and concise items also tend to increase reliability. Test items based upon instructional objectives increase the validity of a test, as well as teach students test-taking skills.

5. Use Assessment Data and Test Results to Guide the Learning Process. There should be a direct correlation among the objectives, test results, and the instructional program. In essence, test results and assessment data should dictate what is to be taught, as well as how it should be taught. Effective teachers use test results to direct and guide the learning process.

Classroom assessment involves more than tests, rubrics, and grades. It should be an integral part of instruction. Carr and Harris (2002) claimed that assessment is the process of quantifying, describing, gathering data about, or giving feedback about performance. Some teachers develop informal assessment techniques to evaluate specific subjects, while others develop plans for the total instructional program. It is the view of the author that a total assessment plan will cover all aspects of the curriculum.

MULTIPLE ASSESSMENT STRATEGIES

A variety of informal assessment strategies should be included in the assessment plan to assess children's learning. Self-assessments, paper and pencil tests, checklists, rating scales, and observations, to name but a few, are assessment strategies that should be included in the plan. Additionally, a variety of assessment strategies are needed to assess different abilities and disabilities in the classroom and to sequence learning steps for children. Teachers should have competencies in choosing appropriate informal assessment techniques needed to objectively evaluate the instructional program, as well as in scoring and grading tests and communicating results to administrators and parents effectively and ethically.

DEVELOPING AN ASSESSMENT SYSTEM

When designing an assessment system the needs, interests, abilities, disabilities, socioeconomic backgrounds, personalities, languages, and learning styles of students must be taken into consideration (Taylor 1999; Delpit 1995). If the aforementioned is not properly conducted and considered, learning is impeded in the classroom. Before any effective assessment is initiated a comprehensive description of pupils should be evident (Goodson 1992). When behavior observed by the teacher is directly related to the traits and characteristics of the pupils, the assessment will be more valid. Additionally, reliability can be established when the teacher looks for and observes consistent patterns of behavior over time.

If properly conducted, assessment information can assist teachers in making informed decisions relevant to the instructional programs. Additionally, teacher assessment should indicate weaknesses and strengths in various subject areas, pupils' readiness, abilities, and disabilities presented within the group, and the type of human and physical resources needed to support the instructional program.

Individuals with disabilities needs must be accommodated in the assessment process as well as in the instructional program. Public Law 94-142 mandates that school districts and teachers identify and assess all children with disabilities. Individuals with disabilities may need accommodations in several areas depending upon their degrees of disability (see chapter 11 for specific details).

REVIEWING SCHOOL RECORDS

Information from school records may be a valuable source for teachers constructing an assessment system or model. Factors such as attendance, patterns of absences, past history of grades, and academic performances in certain subjects can assist teachers when developing an assessment system or model. Many students begin the year with poor grades and then show gradual improvement. For others, the reverse may be true. During the early part of the year, when prior school material is being reviewed, they may do well, with declines in their grades coming as new material is introduced. Also, transition points such as beginning the fourth grade or middle school may cause students problems; the nature and purpose of reading, for example, tends to change when students enter the fourth grade, where reading to learn content becomes more central. Similarly, middle school requires students to assume more responsibility for long-term projects (Hoy and Gregg 1994). These shifts may bring about a noticeable decline in grades for some students.

Test scores are also important to review. Comparing these scores to a student's current classroom performance can indicate that the student's difficulties are new ones, perhaps resulting from some environmental change that needs to be investigated more fully, or the comparison may show that the student has always found a particular skill area to be problematic. "In this situation, the current problems the student is experiencing indicate that the classroom demands have reached a point that the student requires more support to be successful" (Hoy and Gregg 1994).

LOOKING AT STUDENT'S WORK

Often, an initial part of the assessment process includes examining a student's work, either by selecting work samples that can be analyzed to identify academic skills and deficits, or by conducting a portfolio assessment, where folders of the student's work are examined.

When collecting work samples, the teacher selects work from the areas where the student is experiencing difficulty and systematically examines them. The teacher might identify such elements as how the student was directed to do the activity (e.g., orally, in writing), how long it took the student to complete the activity, the pattern of errors (e.g., reversals when writing, etc.), and the pattern of correct answers. Analyzing the student's work in this way can yield valuable insight into the nature of his or her difficulties and suggest possible solutions.

Maintaining portfolios of students' work has become a popular way for teachers to track students' progress. By assembling in one place the body of a student's work, teachers can see how a student is progressing over time, what problems seem to be reoccurring, what concepts are being grasped or not grasped, and what skills are being developed. The portfolio can be analyzed in much the same way as selective work samples and can form the basis for discussions with the student or other teachers about difficulties and successes and for determining what modifications teachers might make in their instruction (Waterman 1994; Wolf 1989).

By considering these factors, teachers should take into account information from school records and student's work to modify and adapt the assessment system to promote success and learning. Some students will need additional time on tasks, others will need additional one-to-one instruction and a variety of physical resources to prepare them to master the assessment strategies. The following guidelines may assist teachers in developing an effective assessment system.

GUIDELINES FOR DEVELOPING TEACHER-MADE TESTS

The following guidelines may be useful for teachers to employ.

1. Identify expected student outcomes and development priorities. Determine the order in which the priorities are to be taught.
2. Develop test items that will require pupils to demonstrate basic knowledge or sub-skills, and the evaluation criteria that will be employed to determine mastery of the skills.
3. Develop test items that are integrated and infused with objectives in the instructional program.
4. Develop competencies in administering, scoring, and interpreting test results to all stakeholders.
5. Use test results to adapt and modify the instructional program, and to change, delete, or upgrade school improvements.
6. Develop skill in using test results to justify a grading pattern.
7. Be knowledgeable about ethical procedures in testing and reporting results.

ASSESSMENT AND CONFERENCES

This is a relatively new concept where students and teachers assess progress or lack of progress made toward achieving stated goals and benchmarks. Sperling (1996), Hawkins (1973), and Wiggins (1993a) refer to this new trend as collaborative assessment. According to these researchers, the teacher presents final topic scores for the student. The student presents his or her scores and evidence to justify the scores. Any disagreement on the scores is discussed in detail. The purpose is to reach some consensus on the scoring. When future tests are developed, assessment conferences should be considered in constructing an assessment model.

1) Assessment Behaviors →	2) Develop Functional → Objectives	3) Assess Objectives →	4) Select Objectives →

5) Select Types of Items →	6) Choose Testing → Formats	7) Analyze Test Items →	8) Select, Adapt, and Modify → Test Items

9) Select Grading Criteria →	10) Develop Ethical → Standards	11) Report Results to → Stakeholders	12) Evaluate the Instructional Program

Figure 1.1. *An Assessment Model*

Figure 1.1 displays a guide for teachers to developing and employing a functional assessment/evaluation plan.

The steps in the model include the following:

- Step 1. Assess the characteristics and learning styles of the children. This step is essential, because the various ways children receive and generate information are important in determining the type of test items and testing formats to include.
- Steps 2 and 3. Develop and assess objectives. These should be stated in objective and measurable terms and directly related to the instructional program.
- Step 4. Select objectives that measure the criteria in Steps 1 through 3.
- Steps 5 and 6. Select the type and format of test items that children can perform without great difficulty.
- Step 7. Analyze test items to determine how well they are meeting the stated objectives.
- Step 8. Select, adapt, and modify test items not meeting the stated objectives.
- Step 9. Select grading standards and criteria before administering the tests.
- Step 10. Develop an ethical standard plan for releasing testing data.
- Step 11. Develop a plan for reporting results to administrators, other teachers, parents, and community agencies associated with educating children.

- Step 12. Evaluate the assessment plan to determine whether or not the instructional program should be modified or changed.

SUMMARY

If assessment results are to be effectively used to gauge to what extent the stated objectives have been achieved, then the assessment process must be properly planned. The teacher must make a decision on what to evaluate and assign priorities in assessing the strengths and weaknesses of students. Informal techniques can be a valuable resource in assessing prior knowledge and the types of human and physical resources needed to achieve the stated objectives. There are a variety of informal techniques that teachers may employ to determine the most appropriate testing format to use with children. Refer to chapters 3 and 11.

In order to effectively guide the instructional program, some type of assessment system should be evident that reflects all of the traits and characteristics of the children, as well as the instructional objectives stated. Multiple assessment strategies should be evident throughout the model as outlined in this chapter, such as school records, information from parents, students' work, portfolios, test scores, observations, and assessing learning styles of children. Evaluations of the model should be conducted frequently to determine if modifications or adaptations are needed in the instructional program. Teachers may need to seek expert opinions within and outside of the school district to assist them. Any assessment system developed should have the endorsement of all stakeholders.

NOTE

1. Refer to George R. Taylor, *Assessing Individuals with Disabilities* (New York: Edwin Mellen Press, 2002).

REFERENCES

Arends, R. I. 2000. *Learning to teach*. New York: McGraw-Hill.
Bloom, B. S., ed. 1956. Taxonomy of educational objectives. *Handbook 1: Cognitive domain*. New York: David McKay.

Carr, J. F., and D. E. Harris. 2002. *Succeeding with standards.* Alexandria, Va.: Association for Supervision and Curriculum Development.

Delpit, L. 1995. *Other people's children: Cultural conflict in the classroom.* New York: The New Press.

Goodson, I. 1992. *Studying teacher's lives: Problems and possibilities.* New York: Teachers College Press.

Gronlund, N. E. 1991. *Constructing achievement tests,* 3rd ed. Englewood Cliffs, N.J.: Prentice Hall.

———. 1998. *Assessment of student achievement,* 6th ed. Boston: Allyn and Bacon.

Hawkins, D. 1973. I, thou, it: The triangular relationship. In C. Silberman, ed., *The open classroom reader.* New York: Random House.

Hoy, C., and N. Gregg. 1994. *Assessment: The special educator's role.* Pacific Grove, Calif.: Brooks/Cole.

Popham, J. W. 2002. *Classroom assessment: What do teachers need to know?* Boston: Allyn and Bacon.

Sperling, D. 1996. Collaborative assessment making high standards a reality for all students. In R. E. Blum and J. A. Arter, eds., *A handbook for student performance assessment in an era of restructuring.* Alexandria, Va.: Association for Supervision and Curriculum Development.

Taylor, G. R. 1999. *Curriculum models and strategies for educating children with disabilities in inclusive classrooms.* Springfield, Ill.: Charles C. Thomas.

———. 2002. *Assessing children with disabilities.* New York: The Edwin Mellen Press.

Waterman, B. B. 1994. Assessing children for the presence of a disability. *National Information Center for Children and Youth with Disabilities 4* (1), 103.

Wiggins, G. 1993a. Assessment authenticity, context, and validity. *Phi Delta Kappan,* 200–214.

Wolf, D. P. 1989. Portfolio assessment: Sampling student work. *Educational Leadership 46* (7), 35–39.

CHAPTER 2

Observational Techniques

Observation may be operantly defined as the act of paying attention to classroom procedures. Instructional procedures are facilitated when the teacher observes pupils' behaviors, social interactions, abilities, disabilities, assignment completions, responses to directions, learning rate, mastery of subject content, and grasp of new concepts, to name but a few (Airasian 2000, pp. 11–12).

The kinds of observations outlined in this text are designed to give educational personnel precise tools for viewing and recording pupils' behaviors in the classroom. Without such tools, observation is subjective.

Systematic observation is an objective means of gathering data that can be employed to understand, correct, or change a situation or individual's behavior. It is an organized way of reviewing for differences that may have positive or negative effects in teaching children. Systematic observation is a necessary requirement for school personnel in directing the education of children. Data generated from systematic observations are also used to make educational decisions and evaluations of instructional and other school-related experiences. Today, many school systems have augmented norm-reference tests and observational techniques because of dissatisfaction with formal observations. Many standardized tests do not provide the means to measure many of our educational goals or to permit comprehensive assessment of programs' effectiveness; consequently, systematic informal assessment may be employed to supplement their use.

TYPES OF OBSERVATIONAL DATA

Observational data may be classified into three general types: (1) narrative, (2) checklist, and (3) rating scales. Narrative data include specimen records, and audio and video tapes. Narrative data must be broken down so that a checklist or rating scale can be employed before they can become effective (see appendix A). Narrative records do not produce usable data until they have been coded or rated systematically (McKinley 1999; Airasian 2001).

Rating scales have been widely used to quantify observational data. In spite of their limitations, rating scales are often the best assessment method available for evaluating many human attributes. Checklists are sets of predefined categories for classifying and tallying live behavior or narrative records. Observer evaluation is minimal, representing a qualitative judgment. Checklists come in many varieties, such as activity logs, event records, and situation responses, to name but a few.

Checklists take a variety of forms and serve a number of purposes. They can be designed for childrens' observations, adults' responses, content, task analysis, activities, events, and so on. They usually require the observer to note whether a particular characteristic is present or absent, while a rating scale requires the observer to record the degree to which a characteristic is present.

OBSERVATIONAL TECHNIQUES

Educators may use check marks to observe the occurrence of the behaviors or simply write yes or no to each behavior. These observational data may be used to determine strengths and weaknesses in various areas and indicate areas where intervention will be needed. As indicated, students may be observed in different settings. The teacher should choose those settings and times where the behaviors are most likely to occur. Certain types of behaviors may manifest themselves at certain times of the day. Several types of recording systems may be used, such as event, duration, and interval recording (Pike and Salend 1995; Swanson and Watson 1989; Wallace, Larsen, and Elksnin 1992; Waterman 1994).

EVENT RECORDING

Event recording involves establishing the frequency of a specific behavior and indicating the number of times a particular behavior occurred per time unit. Teachers record the frequency of students' absences and tardiness, and report the total at the end of the reporting period. Plotting and analyzing these data may indicate trends that suggest ways to change the behavior. Recording events requires some type of recording sheet to note the number of times a behavior occurs. A simple chart as reflected in figure 2.1 may be used.

Teachers may use this form to record the participation of individual children or to record group participation. Names may be recorded for individual children or subjects, and content areas may be recorded for groups. Although frequency or event recording is an appropriate measurement technique for a wide variety of classroom behaviors, it may not always be suitable if the behaviors recorded are continuous rather than divided into discrete responses.

DURATION RECORDING

Duration recording establishes how long a specific behavior persisted. A stopwatch is frequently used to record the amount of time a child engages in the activity or behavior. If sessions are varied in length, the teacher should measure the total session length and divide the total interaction time by it, and the results would be "percentage of time reacting." When more than one observer is concerned with the duration of each interaction, they would start the watch when interaction began, stop it when interaction ceased, record the time accumulated, reset the watch to zero, and wait for the next interaction to occur. When analyzing more than one observer's observation, the process is called "Inter Observer Agreement." It is calculated by taking the cumulative time spent in measuring the behavior, dividing it by the larger total into the smaller

Number of Times Hand Raised	1	2	3	4	5	6	7	8	9	10	11	12	13

Figure 2.1. *Participation in Individual and Group Discussions*

and multiplying by 100. Eighty percent agreement is required for the process. The formula may be expressed as

Total Cumulative Time/Larger Observer's Time/Smaller Observer's Time × 100.

INTERVAL RECORDING

Interval recording establishes the presence or absence of the specific behavior during a time interval. This procedure is sensitive to both the frequency and duration of a behavior. A data sheet should be developed for recording behavior. During each successive interval, the teacher or observer records whether the target behavior has or has not occurred. Frequently, the teacher may use a watch with a sweep second hand to record the passing of the intervals.

Reliability of the technique can be determined by comparing the recording sheets of two independent observers, interval by interval, and dividing the number of agreements by the total number of measurement intervals. The aforementioned formula may be used to validate the process. An advantage of interval recording is that it does not require a behavior analyst to define or classify a precise unit of behavior. Many behaviors can simply be defined as positive or negative by the teacher.

TIME-SAMPLING RECORDING

With this technique observers count the number of times a behavior occurs during a specific time interval. Rather than observe for long periods of time and tally all incidences of the behavior causing concern, the observer divides the observation period into equal time units and observes and tallies behavior only during short periods of time. Based upon the time sampling, predictions can then be made about the student's total behavior. Time intervals need not be consistent; one alternative is simply to decide how many samples are to be taken per session and then to make sure that the correct number is taken.

The recording techniques outlined in this chapter should enable teachers and other school administrators to assess more directly and objectively students' behaviors in all domains. This approach should permit teachers to plan and intervene to correct deficiencies in the instructional program. Teachers should select the type of recording system they deem best for recording behaviors of children. In general, short observations conducted over a period of time is frequently the best method to employ. This approach appears to provide a better sample of the child's behavior. Teachers and educators should rotate the time of observations to reduce getting biased behavior patterns.

INSTRUCTIONAL USE OF OBSERVATIONAL DATA

Kleinsasser (1991) asserts that teacher observations involve the informal conversations and observations of students that teachers make all day, every day. On the other hand, Calfee (1994) and Calfee and Heibert (1991) contend that for observations to be useful, teachers need knowledge and clarity about the skills they are observing. Other researchers articulate that observing the student and his or her environment is an important part of any assessment process. Observations in the classroom and in other settings where the student operates can provide valuable information about his or her academic, motor, communication, or social skills; behaviors that contribute to or detract from learning; and overall attitude or demeanor. Observing the student's environment(s) and his or her behavior within those environments can identify the factors that are influencing the student. For the information from observations to be useful, the team must first define the purpose for the observation and specify the following:

- Where the observation will take place (observing a range of situations where the student operates is recommended);
- When the observation will take place (a number of observations at different times is also important); and
- How the observations will be recorded (Wallace, Larsen, and Elksnin 1992, p. 12).

Observations are a key part of some of the assessment methods that are discussed throughout this text. There are many ways in which to record what is observed; this chapter lists and briefly describes the more common observational methods.

While observations can yield useful information about the student and his or her environments, there are a number of errors that can occur during observations and distort or invalidate the information collected. One source of error may come from the observer—he or she must record accurately, systematically, and without bias. If the observer's general impression of the student influences how he or she rates that student in regard to specific characteristics, the data will be misleading and inaccurate. This can be especially true if the student comes from a background that is different from the majority culture. In such cases, it is important that the observer have an understanding of, and a lack of bias regarding, the student's cultural or language group. Often, multiple observers are used to increase the reliability of the observational information collected. All observers should be fully trained in how to collect information using the specific method chosen (e.g., time sampling using a checklist) and how to remain unobtrusive while observing and recording, so as not to influence the student's behavior. It is also important to observe more than once, in a number of situations or locations, and at various times, and to integrate these data with information gathered through other assessment procedures. Decisions should not be made based upon a narrow range of observational samples (Waterman 1994).

As indicated, students may be observed in different settings. The teacher should choose those settings and times when the behaviors are most likely to occur. Certain types of behaviors may manifest themselves at certain times in the day. According to Marzano (2000), observational data may be scored via rubrics. The teacher assigns a rubric score based on the type of behavior shown. Teachers must construct a system for recording rubrics scores for students, in addition to using several types of recording systems, such as event, duration, and interval recording (Pike and Salend 1995).

SUMMARY

Observation is a prime assessment strategy. It should be an essential part of assessment. There should be some predetermined system or structure to guide the observational process. Of utmost importance, educators define the behavior to be observed as well as the place, time, and duration of the behavior to be observed. Once the educator has selected the types of behavior to be observed, it will be necessary to develop or use some type of recording instrument to record the observations. Check marks may be used to record the occurrences of the behaviors by simply writing yes or no to each behavior. These observational data may be used to determine strengths and weaknesses in various areas where intervention will be needed.

Observation checklists take a variety of forms and serve a number of purposes as reflected throughout this chapter. They vary sharply in coverage and the target object for investigation.

A common weakness of comprehensive observation systems is their tendency to be somewhat content free; they focus directly on process description. A second weakness is the rather limited specificity of the categories that relate to a given dimension. If a single observer must code a number of dimensions, the number of categories per dimension is often as few as two and seldom greater than six or seven. Single dimension scales need to be used to generate more precise data about narrowly focused types of behavior.

REFERENCES

Airasian, P. W. 2000. *Assessment in the classroom: A concise approach*. New York: McGraw-Hill.

———. 2001. *Classroom assessment: Concepts and applications*. New York: McGraw-Hill.

Calfee, R. C. 1994. *Implications for cognitive psychology for authentic assessment and instructions*. (Tech. Report No. 69). Berkeley: National Center for the Study of Writing, University of California.

Calfee, R. C., and E. H. Heibert. 1991. Classroom assessment of reading. In R. Barr, M. Kamil, P. Mosenthal, and P. D. Pearson, eds., *Handbook of Research on Reading,* 2nd ed. New York: Longman.

Kleinsasser, A. 1991. *Rethinking assessment: Who's the expert?* Paper presented at the Casper Outcomes Conference, Casper, Wyo.

Marzano, R. J. 2000. *Transforming classroom grading*. Alexandria, Va.: Association for Supervision and Curriculum Development.

McKinley, J. 1999. Observational assessment: Validating what teachers see in the classroom. *Education Update* 41, 5–6.

Pike, K., and S. Salend. 1995. Authentic assessment strategies. *Teaching Exceptional Children* 28 (1), 15–19.

Swanson, H. C., and B. L. Watson. 1989. *Educational and psychological assessment of exceptional children,* 2nd ed. Columbus, Ohio: Merrill Publishing Company.

Wallace, G., S. C. Larsen, and L. K. Elksnin. 1992. *Educational assessment of learning problems: Testing for teaching.* Boston: Allyn and Bacon.

Waterman, B. B. 1994. *Assessing children in the presence of a disability.* Washington, D.C.: National Information Center for Children and Youth with Disabilities.

CHAPTER 3

Developing Objective Types of Test Items

Assessment is a process of collecting relevant information on individuals in order to make valid decisions about them in areas of learning and human functioning. It is a multifaceted process, which involves more than the use of standardized or informal tests. The process includes assessing individuals in a variety of mental, physical, and social tasks. This text is designed to address the use of tests to make sound educational decisions, which may be used by individualized education teams to make valid instructional decisions (Taylor 1997; Salvia and Ysseldyke 1998; Witt, Elliott, Daly, Gresham, and Kramer 1998).

MAJOR TYPES OF ASSESSMENT DEVICES AND STRATEGIES

Several types of assessment devices and strategies are used to make decisions relevant to student's abilities and disabilities. They are too numerous to be listed in this chapter. The reader seeking additional information is referred to any basic book on assessment. The purpose of this chapter is to overview the educational use of informal assessment information, for evaluating children with exceptionalities, including techniques such as observation, portfolio assessment, self assessment, and various types of tests employed to assess human behavior (McLoughlin and Lewis 1991; Browder 1991).

Objective-type tests may be used to supplement or compare results from standardized tests. They also may be employed where standardized tests are not adequate for reasons of content, difficulty, scope, or sensitive cultural materials. Teacher-made tests are based on objectives of the course. A teacher-made test is greatly improved when the teacher knows the principles that govern the writing of objective-type items and assessing them in examinations. One of the first things a teacher should consider in constructing a test is the type of test format to be employed, as well as the objectives of the course. There are several types of testing formats: (1) true-false, (2) multiple-choice, (3) matching, (4) completion, (5) essay, (6) questionnaires, (7) interviews, and (8) inventories and subject matter tests (Airasian, 2001). The type of format chosen will greatly depend upon the disabling conditions of the children being tested. For example, an essay type may not be suited for a child with cerebral palsy. Several adaptations and modifications may need to be made in the testing command and response. These major concerns are addressed later in the chapter.

The aforementioned testing formats can be scored in various ways. In some instances the raw scores of correct responses can simply be counted up and a letter grade assigned. In other cases, points can be assigned and converted to letter grades. One of the newest ways to score teacher-made objective tests is through the application of rubrics (refer to chapter 5 for special strategies, also see appendix B).

PLANNING OBJECTIVE-TYPE TESTS

The first step in planning a teacher-made test is to write specifications for the test. The purpose must be clearly articulated. Steps include arranging items in order of difficulty, preparing directions for administering the test, setting time limits, conducting an item analysis, constructing a scoring system, and establishing reliability and validity for the test. Specifications need to be written for each subject area tested. Subject areas will determine the nature and extent of the specification written. Teachers may need some assistance in completing the aforementioned steps, especially in conducting an item analysis and establishing reliability and validity. It is recommended that teachers consult with a psychology research and evaluation department at a local university or with the school system research and evaluation department.

A second step for teachers is to decide on the type of objective test items to be used. This is explained in greater detail later in the chapter. In choosing a testing format, teachers should determine the following factors:

- A description of the test
- The purpose for giving the test
- The nature and extent of students' disabilities
- The number of items to be presented
- Timing of the test
- A pre-item analysis of the test items, eliminating those items that are too easy or difficult, and rewriting items based upon the analysis.

A third step is to arrange the items in order of difficulty from easy to hard. For many children with disabilities, a series of easy items may be infused with hard ones to develop confidence and self-esteem.

A fourth step is to prepare directions for administering the test. Directions should come at the beginning of each part. The time limit should be set based upon the ages, and other abilities and disabilities of the children. For some disabled children, accommodations may need to be made, such as increasing the time for them to complete the items, or reading the items to them and recording their responses.

A fifth step is that teachers should be skilled in using and communicating assessment results when making decisions about individual students' instructional programs relevant to school and society.

A sixth step is for teachers to develop skillfully valid pupil grading procedures, which use results from pupil assessments. Teachers using this standard will have justification for their grading system, which will be based upon assessment data (Marzano 2000).

A seventh step is to recognize unethical, illegal, and otherwise inappropriate assessment methods and use of assessment information. In order to use the standard effectively, teachers will have to be knowledgeable about local and state laws governing ethical standards relating to testing and assessment (Airasian 2001). Major testing formats are described below.

TRUE-FALSE TEST ITEMS

True-false test items comprise a series of questions that instructs the student to mark true or false for each response. In some instances, the student may be instructed to mark "yes" or "no" for each response. There is an opportunity for students to guess on true-false tests, thus, the teacher should be as objective as possible when constructing them.

There are several advantages in using true-false tests (Ebel 1970; Airasian 2001):

1. They may be used with many types of materials.
2. They are easily scored.
3. They are objective.
4. They are simple to construct.
5. They provide a wide sampling of materials in a short space.
6. They are time savers, and may be frequently used.
7. They provide easy directions for children to follow.

There are major disadvantages in using true-false tests:

1. They may be confusing to students.
2. They are open to guessing.
3. Some information cannot be stated as absolutely true or false.
4. They may become collections of detached and unrelated bits of information.
5. They may stress rote memory instead of comprehension.

CONSTRUCTING TRUE-FALSE TESTS

In order to minimize some of the aforementioned disadvantages of true-false tests, teachers should: (1) place the symbols "T" and "F" after each question and instruct the children to circle the appropriate response; (2) make the number of true items equal to the number of false ones. The teacher may use the following format for scoring the test (right-wrong). This process assists in correcting for guessing; (3) write items as objectively as possible, leaving personal views and tricky questions out; (4) avoid using questions which are partly true and partly false; (5) avoid using verbatim questions; (6) avoid the use of absolute words, such as *all, none, always, never, every.*

True-false testing appears to be the fastest way to cover a wide range of information. When used with test information, they can be valuable in assessing the abilities of children. These items appear to be easy to write, however, writing false statements may constitute a challenge for teachers because they must be plausible enough to attract students who do not know the content. An additional weakness of true-false test items is that they are susceptible to evaluation error because of student guesses (Marzano 2000).

MULTIPLE-CHOICE TESTS

Multiple-choice test items are widely used in both formal and informal tests. They are one of the most flexible of objective form tests. Test items consist of a statement, phrase, or word followed by several responses, only one of which is correct. Multiple-choice items may be designed to assess a variety of information, such as comprehension, understanding concepts, applying principles, interpreting data, and assessing knowledge in most subject areas (Haladya 1992).

There are several advantages for teachers using multiple-choice test items. Principally the advantages include:

1. Answers are objective and easily scored.
2. Items may be written to measure critical thinking skills, such as analysis, synthesis, and evaluation.
3. Choices are given to assist in minimizing guessing.
4. Items may be written to measure knowledge, comprehension, and application.

Despite these wide uses, there are inherited disadvantages:

1. Many items are too factual and stress too much recall and memory of specific facts.
2. Several responses may be correct or nearly correct.
3. Clues may significantly impact the response chosen.

4. Distractors may lead to incorrect responses. They should not be confusing.

CONSTRUCTING MULTIPLE-CHOICE ITEMS

Constructing multiple-choice items is a complex process involving an understanding of and competencies in the subject area being measured or assessed, as well as the strategies listed below:

1. Teachers should vary the position of the alphabet denoting the correct response. In essence, place the right answer in various positions. The formula for scoring is Score = Right − (Wrong). This formula is used to correct for guessing. The number of options must be the same in each item if the above formula is to be used.
2. Do not include responses that are so unrelated to the question that the answer can easily be recognized.
3. Do not list incorrect answers that appear true enough to be the correct answer, such as partially true answers.
4. Do not provide clues that will give away the correct answer, such as having the right answer being consistency long or short, or having one option or alphabet letter being consistently correct.
5. Items followed by a series of options communicate more clearly than items in which the answers are imbedded in the statement.

MULTIPLE-RESPONSE ITEMS

Unlike multiple-choice items, multiple-response items require a number of possible answers, several of which may be correct. The advantages and disadvantages for constructing those items are similar to those discussed above, in Multiple-Choice Tests (Haladya 1997).

MATCHING ITEMS

When constructing matching items, the teacher matches a list of words, names, or phrases against another list. Matching items may be used to test the relationships between statements. One major disadvantage of matching items is that they may measure memory rather than compre-hension. Other factors should be considered in constructing matching items, such as

1. Limiting the number of items in the list; five or seven items are recommended. Long lists require too much time for students to complete the items.
2. Choosing information from one academic area, so that a given item in Column 1 has several matches in Column 2. Give clear di-rections for matching the items.
3. Arranging names in alphabetical order and dates and numbers in sequence order to save the student time in completing the test.
4. As in multiple choice items, teachers should refrain from giving clues.

These items permit teachers to cover a great deal of information in a short time. Matching is well suited to quickly survey specific information when specified information is needed. Some of the same strategies em-ployed in constructing multiple-choice items apply to matching items.

COMPLETION ITEMS

Children are instructed to fill in blanks to complete the meaning of the sentence or phrase. Completing these items requires recalling specific facts and the ability to comprehend overall relationships. These types of items are not suited for many children with disabilities because of the limitations imposed by their disabilities. Teachers should consider this factor before administering test items of this nature.

When writing completion type items, the following are recom-mended:

1. Do not copy information directly from the text; rephrase the in-formation to reduce the reliance on rote memory. Questions should be designed to promote critical thinking skills.
2. Limit the number of blanks children are required to complete. Too many blanks will frequently confuse children.
3. Scoring is more objective if words rather than phrases are deleted.

4. Make all blanks the same size to avoid clues about the length of the correct word.
5. When there is more than one correct answer, provide for them in the scoring key.
6. Guard against giving clues to children by making sure completions do not depend upon grammatical form or textbook expressions.

THE ESSAY

The essay is a widely used test in most subject areas. These tests are designed to assess understanding, organization, and interpretation of information. The essay was one of the first forms of assessment used in public education (Durm 1993). In constructing essay questions, teachers should avoid questions that ask a question or ask for a specific name or location. Questions beginning with such words as "discuss," "evaluate," "outline," and "explain" usually get a mass of details, of which many are not relevant. The form and construction of the question are important.

Objectivity of the essay question can be improved when short answers are employed and responses have been restricted. Recall and problem situation questions may make essay questions more objective and easier to score. In recall questions, answers are limited to short statements or paragraphs. These questions are similar to completion type questions. Problem situation questions focus on some important aspect or situation. Scoring the essay test objectively has always created a problem for teachers due chiefly to students being given options in their responses and the scoring criteria being interpreted differently by teachers. Unified instructions and scoring will do much to reduce subjectivity in administering and scoring essay questions and examinations. The essay can be a valuable test for assessing abilities in school-related subjects when the above recommendations are adhered to.

Essay items can also be used to determine a student's communication, thinking, and reasoning skills.

Some essay tests may be called "performance tasks." These items require the application of knowledge. However, the reader is cautioned to be aware that not all performance tasks are essays and some performance tasks do not require written responses, whereas all essays do. Research findings by Marzano, Pickering, and McTighe (1993) support this premise and they further articulate that, like essay items, one of the most powerful aspects of performance tasks is that they can be employed to assess a variety of forms of knowledge.

QUESTIONNAIRES

Questionnaires consist of a set of questions designed to gather information to fit different formats such as surveys, checklists, rating scales, multiple-choice, matching, completing, and true-false statements. Questionnaires are designed to collect specific information from students. Little training is needed in constructing questionnaires. The only requirement is knowledge of the content being solicited. They are easily administered and scored and may be useful for teachers gathering information to employ in the instructional program.

INTERVIEWS

For many children with disabilities an alternate means must be available for collecting information other than questionnaires. Their disabilities frequently prohibit them from responding to questionnaires appropriately. Interviews may be substituted to elicit information. The teacher may control the length and time and provide directions during the interviewing process. Frequently, teachers need detailed information that students cannot provide. Parents and other professionals must be interviewed to secure the necessary information. The validity of information secured from interviews greatly depends upon the accuracy of the information being provided by the interviewer. Teachers must be aware and proceed with caution when interpreting information.

INVENTORIES AND SUBJECT MATTER TESTS

Inventories and subject matter tests may be used to assess a variety of skills in curricula areas for children with disabilities. They provide information on children's present levels of functioning within the curriculum. Inventories may be developed by the teacher or purchased commercially for many subject areas. In designing inventories and sub-ject matter tests, teachers should be knowledgeable about

1. The curriculum area being assessed;
2. Developmentally appropriate skills;
3. Breaking tasks or skills into small manageable parts;
4. Preparing test items for each sub-test of the curriculum being assessed;
5. Adapting and modifying the number of test items based upon the disabilities of the children; and
6. Sequencing the test items from easiest to more difficult degrees of difficulty (Taylor 1999).

Writing specifications for inventory and subject matter tests must also be considered. The purpose of the test must be clearly articulated and specifications for the test developed as discussed in developing other types of informal tests. Steps include arranging items in order of diffi-culty, preparing directions for administering the test, setting the time limit, conducting an item analysis, constructing a scoring system, and establishing the reliability and validity of the test. Educators may need professional assistance in conducting an item analysis and establishing the reliability and validity of a test. Several techniques for establish-ing the validity and reliability of informal test items have been high-lighted throughout the text.

When constructing objective-type test items, teachers not only should be aware of ethical standards, they should also be aware of the legal mandates concerning accommodations for children with disabili-ties. States are required to have a list of acceptable published accom-modations that teachers can employ when constructing, administering, and scoring objective test items.

ASSESSMENT ACCOMMODATIONS

New regulations of the Individuals with Disabilities Education Act (IDEA) mandate that students with exceptionalities are to be in-cluded in general state and district-wide assessment programs with accommodations if needed. An assessment accommodation is an alteration in the way a test is given. It is designed to permit students with exceptionalities to show what they know without the impediment of the exceptionality (Elliott, Ysseldyke, Thurlow, and Erickson 1998). In essence, accommodations make the field level for students with exceptionalities.

The new IDEA makes it abundantly clear that school districts must describe in the IEP what accommodations will or will not be used. Thurlow, Elliott, and Ysseldyke (1998) have developed a checklist for teachers, educators, and the IEP team to employ when making decisions to determine what accommodations are valid in altering the testing format in norm-referenced tests. Accommodations may take many forms, such as (1) extending time, (2) reducing stimulus response, and (3) using assistive devices. Alternative assessment is another technique that educators can employ in adapting and modifying assessment devices.

SUMMARY

Several types of objective-type, teacher-made tests are summarized in this chapter. Advantages and disadvantages of their use are cited. Teachers should choose the formats that best meet their objectives as well as the abilities and disabilities of the class. By combining some of the test formats, they can provide a comprehensive assessment of students' abilities and disabilities in several areas of functioning.

Regardless of the type of test format selected, teachers should

1. Give clear and concise directions to children;
2. Provide accommodations for students who may need them;
3. Avoid ambiguous statements;
4. Not give clues when writing test items relevant to correct responses;
5. Write clear test items and avoid any complex syntax;
6. Use vocabulary on the level of the students;
7. Minimize negatives and double concepts items;
8. Describe the tasks for students; and
9. Write uniform test items.

REFERENCES

Airasian, P. W. 2001. *Classroom assessment: Concepts and applications,* 4th ed. New York: McGraw-Hill.

Browder, D. M. 1991. *Assessment of individuals with severe disabilities: An applied behavior approach to life skills assessment,* 2nd ed. Baltimore, Md.: Brookes.

Durm, M. W. 1993. ANA is not an A is not a A: A history of grading. *The Educational Forum* 57, 294–97.

Ebel, R. L. 1970. The case for true-false test items. *School Review* 78, 373–89.

Elliott, J., J. Ysseldyke, M. Thurlow, and R. Erickson. 1998. What about assessment and accountability? Practical implications for educators. *Teaching Exceptional Children* 31 (1), 20–27.

Haladya, T. M. 1992. The effectiveness of several multiple-choice formats. *Applied Measurement in Education* 5, 73–88.

———. 1997. *Writing test items to evaluate higher order thinking.* Boston: Allyn and Bacon.

Marzano, R. J. 2000. *Transforming classroom grading.* Alexandria, Va.: Association for Supervision and Curriculum Development.

Marzano, R. J., D. J. Pickering, and J. McTighe. 1993. *Assessing student outcomes: Performance assessment using the dimension of learning model.* Alexandria, Va.: Association for Supervision and Curriculum Development.

McLoughlin, J., and R. Lewis. 1991. *Assessing special students: Strategies and procedures,* 3rd ed. Columbus, Ohio: Charles E. Merrill.

Salvia, J., and J. E. Ysseldyke. 1998. *Assessment.* Boston: Houghton-Mifflin.

Shavelson, R. J., and G. P. Baxter. 1992. What we've learned about assessing hands-on science. *Educational Leadership* 49, 20–25.

Shavelson, R. J., X. Gao, and G. P. Baxter. 1993. *Sampling variability of performance assessments* (Report No. 361). Santa Barbara: University of California, National Center for Research in Evaluation, Standards and Student Testing.

Taylor, G. R. 1997. *Curriculum strategies: Social skills intervention for young African American males.* Westport, Conn.: Praeger.

———. 1999. *Curriculum models and strategies for educating individuals with disabilities in inclusive classrooms.* Springfield, Ill.: Charles C. Thomas.

Thurlow, M. L., J. L. Elliott, and J. E. Ysseldyke. 1998. *Testing students with disabilities: Practical strategies for complying with district and state requirements.* Thousand Oaks, Calif.: Corwin Press.

Witt, J. C., S. N. Elliott, E. J. Daly III, F. M. Gresham, and J. Kramer. 1998. *Assessment of at-risk and special needs children.* New York: McGraw-Hill.

CHAPTER 4

Preparing Pupils for Informal Tests

Much controversy exists concerning test preparation for pupils. Questions such as the nature and types of test preparations to be employed have frequently been reported in the professional literature (Canner et al. 1991; Popham 1991; Airasian 2001; and Taylor 2002). These authors uniformly agree that specific ethical and appropriate guidelines should be developed for preparing pupils to take tests. Application of these guidelines in test preparation will assist pupils in mastering the content taught. Additionally, informal tests constructed should request that pupils respond to tasks or test items similar to those taught during instruction. Specific strategies are given in chapter 9 for infusing and integrating objectives, instruction, and the test in teaching and in assessing the extent pupils have mastered what they have been taught.

ETHICAL CONSIDERATIONS

Test preparations given to pupils must meet appropriate and ethical guidelines. Teachers must draw a distinction between teaching basic concepts related to the test and teaching test items *specifically* targeted to the test. When the latter is conducted, there are serious, unethical, and inappropriate test preparation practices violations. These violations, if proven, may be severe, resulting in reprimands and sometimes dismissal of education personnel. Teaching test-taking skills implies that the teacher teach pupils the general concepts, understandings, skills, knowledges, and processes associated in applying appropriately and correctly to the test. This approach is considered to be a valid and recommended practice. Teachers and related school personnel involved with testing and assessing pupils should have a moral and ethical responsibility in not teaching the exact items on a test (Joint Advisory Committee 1993). Canner et al. (1991) and Popham (1991) have provided guidelines for teachers to use in teaching test preparation practices to pupils, both ethical and unethical.

ETHICAL GUIDELINES

1. Teach pupils general test-taking skills and concepts that will improve their understanding of testing practices. Basic concepts and skills germane to the subject content may be used to solve problems in science, mathematics, or any basic subject. An example in science may include the following concept, "Matter can neither be created nor destroyed." This concept may be demonstrated through burning a candle and asking, What is happening to the candle? Is matter being destroyed? What is happening to matter? Was the candle or matter in the candle destroyed? Use the above concept to answer the questions. Employing conceptual information can be used to answer or solve problems in any academic area, and test items which include certain concepts should be reviewed by teachers, modeling specific activities and giving children the opportunity to demonstrate the skills.

2. Provide a review for children, including stressing important points, making sure that objectives are well understood by children, providing practice on items with different levels of difficulty and skills, and giving children the opportunity to ask questions concerning concepts that are not clear, as well as clarifying issues and content. In order to maintain ethical standards, educators should make sure that review content is not the same as the test items or content.

3. Confine instruction to the objectives that will be tested, providing that they do not prepare pupils for specific test items in the test. It is ethical for educators to give pupils drills on the objectives similar to those in the test prior to testing, as this will assist in preparing pupils to respond more readily to test items. Preparation for the test may take many forms, such as using the experi-

ences of the children, summarizing key components of the objectives, and constructing a review test with similar test items. These strategies should be designed for pupils to review behaviors previously learned.

4. Discuss the difference between various testing formats. When unfamiliar testing formats are used, teachers should provide instruction and information to children. See chapter 3 for different testing formats. Opportunities should be provided for the teacher to model and demonstrate how to respond to the different formats, as well as entertain and answer questions posed by pupils. These activities will assist in reducing frustrations when pupils are responding to various testing formats. Teachers should provide practice experiences using the testing formats that will be included in the test.

5. Schedule the test at an appropriate time. Teachers are often confronted with this dilemma. The following recommendations are given for teachers to implement:

- Don't test when important schoolwide activities are planned.
- Don't test when pupils are returning from vacations.
- Don't test the day a teacher returns from a prolong period of absence.
- Don't authorize a substitute teacher to test children (because the substitute teacher may not be familiar with administering the test or the pupils may not be familiar with the substitute teacher and not perform at their best level).

Provide pupils with information relevant to the test. The more information given to pupils concerning the test, the better the test results will be. Provide information such as the content to be covered, administration of the test, types of questions, and format to be presented in the test. When relative information is provided to pupils, their self-confidence is improved. This improvement can but only improve their test scores. Airasian (2001) believes that a teacher must inform pupils about the characteristics of a test well in advance of its administration (p. 162). It is incumbent upon all school personnel testing and assessing pupils that they be knowledgeable and practice appropriate and ethical test-taking practices.

UNETHICAL CONSIDERATIONS AND GUIDELINES

Frequently, teachers are not aware of unethical practices in test preparation. Many unintentionally provide clues and information that may significantly influence the results. Canner et al. (1991) have produced a set of guidelines under the auspices of The National Council of Measurement in Education Task Force and listed inappropriate and unethical guidelines for test preparation. They are

1. Focusing instruction only on the tasks or items and formats used for the test.
2. Using examples during instruction that are identical to test items or tasks.
3. Giving pupils practice taking tests items.

In addition to the above inappropriate and unethical practices, teachers should not

1. Include information on the test that has not been covered in the instructional program. It is unfair to test pupils on information they have not been taught. This may account for lower test scores, which may not reflect the true abilities of the pupils. Effective instruction should be followed up by a review that permits pupils a chance to ask questions and demonstrate skills and behaviors that will be tested and indicate how well they have learned what has been taught.
2. Overlook the importance of test length when constructing test items. Test length should be based upon several factors, including the age, attention span, abilities, and disabilities of the pupils. In essence, the length of test items should not be above the abilities of the pupils.
3. Forget to provide accommodations in constructing test items for pupils who need them. Basic accommodations strategies are summarized in chapter 1. Due to the variety of disabled individuals who need accommodations, teachers should not be expected to know all of the strategies, however, they should be aware of resources to consult. Price and Nelson (1999) are an excellent re-

source to consult. They have listed a summary of common disabilities and accommodations that educators can employ in the instructional program.

4. Provide clues that may lead to the pupil choosing through guessing the correct option, such as familiar words, options that are longer, options that are more precisely stated, and unlikely choices that do not attach smoothly to the stem of an item.

5. Schedule testing at inappropriate times. An inappropriate time may be defined as when events may significantly distract pupils, such as schoolwide events, vacations, prolonged absences of the teacher, and extended illnesses, or family related problems. Any of these events can have a profound effect on the results. Teachers should reschedule testing when any of the above occurs in order to permit pupils to demonstrate their best work.

Various school districts will have standards in which they consider inappropriate or unethical practices in testing. Teachers should check with the appropriate administrative office responsible and become familiar with the standards. It is also recommended that in-service workshops be conducted to apprise teachers and other educators of inappropriate and unethical testing practices (Marso and Pigge 1989).

Popham (2002) has provided two basic evaluative guidelines that teachers may employ to determine the effectiveness of given test preparation practices. They are more general than the previously mentioned guidelines under ethical practices. The two general ethics guidelines fall under Professional Ethics and Educational Defensibility.

PROFESSIONAL ETHICS

This guideline states that "No test-preparation practice should violate the ethical norms of the education profession" (p. 308). There is some similarity between ethical standards articulated by Airasian (2001) and Popham (2002). They both agree that it is incumbent upon teachers to avoid test-preparation practices that are unethical and include such practices as theft, cheating, lying, and giving pupils clues to test items, to name but a few (Cannell 1989; Cizek 1999). When the public becomes aware of the teachers' unethical test-taking practices, confidence in the teaching profession is eroded and the long-term effects may be indicated in a decline in public support for the schools.

EDUCATIONAL DEFENSIBILITY

This guideline specifies that "No test-preparation practice should increase students' test scores without simultaneously increasing students' mastery of the assessment domain tested" (Popham 2002, 309). Popham wrote that this standard emphasizes the importance of engaging in instructional practices that are in the educational best interests of students (p. 309). In essence, it is unethical for teachers to report high scores on a test while the domain being tested does not reflect the student's mastery of the content. If test-preparation practices are appropriately conducted, both the preparation and the content being tested should show an increase. On the other hand, an inappropriate test-preparation may raise performance on the test but not students' mastery of the content. Consequently, inappropriate test-preparation practices cannot be defended educationally, because they reflect an inaccurate picture of students' performances (Phillips 1996).

SUMMARY

Most informal tests are constructed by teachers and are based upon objectives of the instructional program. Like all tests, informal tests are principally designed to test the outcomes of instruction. Teachers must become aware of the test construction, administration, and evaluation. Nothing is more important than using appropriate and ethical standards in testing (Strike and Soltis, 1991).

In preparing pupils for taking tests, teachers should not give pupils practice in taking the actual test (Joint Committee on Testing Practices 1988). This practice may invalidate the test results. Airasian (2001) states that instruction should be focused on the general skills and knowledge teachers want pupils to learn in a subject area, not on the specific question that will be asked about those areas on the test (p. 163).

REFERENCES

Airasian, P. W. 2001. *Classroom assessment: Concepts and application*. Boston: McGraw-Hill.

Cannell, J. J. 1989. *How public education cheats on standardized achievement tests*. Albuquerque, N.M.: Friends of Education.

Canner, J. 1991. *Regaining trust: Enhancing the credibility of school testing programs*. Xerox. National Council on Measurement in Education Task Force.

Canner, J., T. Fisher, J. Fremer, T. Haladyna, J. Hall, W. Mehrens, C. Perlman, E. Roeber, and P. Sandifer. 1991. *Regaining trust: Enhancing the credibility of school programs*. (Xerox.) National Council on Measurement in Education Task Force.

Cizek, G. J. 1999. *Cheating on tests: How to do it, detect it, and prevent it*. Mahwah, N.J.: Lawrence Erlbaum.

Joint Advisory Committee. 1993. *Principle for fair student assessment practices for education in Canada*. Edmonton, Canada: University of Alberta.

Joint Committee on Testing Practices. 1988. *Code of fair testing practices in education*. Washington, D.C.: American Psychological Association.

Marso, R. N., and F. L. Pigge. 1989. Elementary classroom teachers' testing needs and proficiencies: Multiple assessment and in-service training priorities. *Educational Review* 13, 1–17.

Phillips, S. E. 1996. Legal defensibility of standards: Issues and policy perspectives. *Educational Measurement Issues and Practices* 15 (2), 5–13, 19.

Popham, J. W. 1991. Appropriateness of teachers' test preparation practices. *Educational Measurement: Issues and Practice* 10 (4), 12–15.

———. 2002. *Classroom assessment: What do teachers need to know?* Boston: Allyn and Bacon.

Price, K. M., and K. L. Nelson. 1999. *Daily planning for today's classroom*. Belmont, Calif.: Wadsworth Publishing.

Strike, K., and J. Soltis. 1991. *The ethic of teaching*. New York: Teachers College Press.

Taylor, G. R. 2002. *Assessing students with disabilities*. New York: Edwin Mellen Press.

CHAPTER 5

Performance Assessment

Airasian (2001) has given an operational definition of performance assessment that can easily be validated in the classroom. He states that assessments occur when pupils carry out an activity or produce a product in order to demonstrate their learning. Meyer (1992) voices that the terms *performance* and *authentic assessment* are often used interchangeably but do not mean the same thing. He states that, in a performance assessment, the student completes or demonstrates the same behavior that the assessor desires to measure. There is a minimal degree, if any, of inference involved. For example, if the behavior to be measured is writing, the student writes. The student does not complete multiple-choice questions about sentences and paragraphs, which instead measures the student's ability to proofread other people's writing and requires a high degree of inference about the student's ability to write.

In an authentic assessment, the student not only completes or demonstrates the desired behavior but also does it in a real-life context. "Real life" may be in terms of the student (for example, the classroom) or it may be an adult expectation. The significant criterion for the authenticity of a writing assignment might be that the locus of control rests with the student; that is, the student determines the topic, the time allocated, the pacing, and the conditions under which the writing sample is generated.

Meyer (1992) affirms that educators should be cognizant of the differences between performances and authentic assessments for the following reasons:

1. When reading professional publications and attending professional meetings, educators must determine whether presenters understand the difference between the two terms.
2. Educators must become informed consumers when purchasing assessment materials being marked as performance or authentic assessments.
3. When planning assessment strategies, educators must be informed enough to determine what types of assessments will best meet the stated objectives and promote student learning.

Wiggins (1992) makes no distinction between the two terms; he infers that performance assessments permit pupils to *demonstrate* what they can do in real situations, rather than *articulate* how a task or skill should be completed. The latter skill is usually shown through various types of objective test items and is described in chapter 3.

According to Bartz, Anderson-Robinson, and Hillman (1994), paper and pencil tests such as essays and other response items may provide a final product demonstrating how pupils think as well as how they perform on the test. Paper and pencil tests of this nature are considered forms of performance assessments. Performance assessment activities can be conducted during instruction, demonstrating the use of equipment, or performing or demonstrating a task in any school-related activity, as long as the teacher stipulates the conditions in which the performance is shown and assessed.

Performance assessment has had a long history of use in the classroom. Pupils have been required to describe and demonstrate evidence of performance skills by applying prior knowledge (Meyer 1992; Madaus and O'Dwyer 1999). Some of the common performance assessments that have been used in the schools fall under the following domains:

1. Communication Skills: These skills are demonstrated through writing essays, giving speeches, and following spoken directions.

2. Psychomotor Skills: Involve such activities as setting up laboratory equipment, using scissors, holding a pencil, and dissecting a frog.
3. Athletic Activity: Activities include shooting free throws, catching a ball, hopping, and swimming the crawl.
4. Concept Acquisition: Tasks include constructing open and closed circuits, selecting proper tools for shop tasks, identifying unknown chemical substances, and generalizing from experimental data.
5. Affective Skills: These skills involve sharing toys, working in cooperative groups, obeying school rules, and maintaining self-control (Airasian 2001).

The use of performance assessments in the schools may be attributed to several factors. First, the most important reason for their improved status is that several states have mandated their use as part of formal statewide assessment programs. Second, school districts have placed higher value on problem solving, higher level thinking, and real-world reasoning skills, which in turn has increased the use of performance assessment strategies to demonstrate pupils' learning. A third reason may be attributed to the fact that performance assessment can provide another avenue for pupils with disabilities and other pupils who do poorly on certain tests an alternate way to demonstrate mastery of skills (Ryan and Miyasaka 1995; Madaus and O'Dwyer 1999).

Since most schools expect students to show proficiency in communication skills, reading, writing, and speaking are the most common types of performance assessments used. The other four types, not as common, are used to determine pupils' understanding of concepts taught and to evaluate their abilities to apply skills taught in the domains of psychomotor abilities, affective skills, athletic activities, and concept acquisition. Pupils are taught to carry out all these performance assessments under the four domains through many repetitions. Observational techniques are the major assessment strategy used to denote areas showing weakness or mastery of the skill or product evaluated. Because of lack of development or disabilities in certain areas, performance assessments can be effectively used with early childhood programs and pupils with disabilities to assess progress or the lack of it.

COMPONENTS OF PERFORMANCE ASSESSMENT

Airasian (2001); Fager, Blake, and Impara (1997); Stiggins (1997); Arter (1999); and Marzano, Pickering, and McTighe (1993) agree that when developing performance assessments it is essential that the following features be included: (1) purpose of the assessment, (2) performance criteria, (3) a setting to observe the performance, and (4) a score to describe the performance.

Purpose of Assessment

Performance assessments serve many purposes in the classroom. Teachers use them for assigning grades, diagnosing learning difficulties, developing portfolios of pupils' work, recognizing important steps in demonstrating a performance, and sharing pupils' work with parents. In essence, they can provide objective information relevant to pupils' strengths and weaknesses when performance criteria are stated in terms of reasonable and observable behavior.

Performance Criteria

Performance criteria denote the specific skills a pupil should demonstrate to carry out a performance. Teachers must first decide what process or product will be observed. In some cases both process and product can be assessed. Performance criteria are essential to successful performance assessment, and broad areas such as using an instrument, participating in a sport, and obeying school rules must be broken down into specific skills before they can be successfully assessed. The complexity of performance criteria necessitates that educators should have training in order to assist their pupils on performance assessment. In essence, teachers should be trained to assist pupils in identifying criteria that are necessary to perform the task. Performance criteria should be stated in clear and concise terms that students understand. Additionally, the teacher should share, explain, and if needed model the performance criteria to the pupils. These techniques are highly recommended for many individuals with disabilities.

Teachers should exercise caution in developing performance criteria. Different teachers may have different performance criteria, based on the needs and interests of their pupils. Most school performances and products can be broken down into specific criteria. Teachers rarely have time or the resources to evaluate and assess numerous specific performance criteria for individual pupils. In order for performance criteria to be effective, teachers must identify the essential criteria associated with the tasks or products. Most teachers can successfully manage six to twelve performance criteria.

Identifying performance criteria is never completed; it is an ongoing process where criteria are identified and modified as needs and circumstances dictate. For example, after a teacher has observed a performance, it may be necessary to revise the criteria by using distinct categories. The following guidelines advocated by Airasian (2001) are noteworthy, and teachers should consider using them in developing performance criteria:

- Select the performance or product to be assessed and either perform it yourself or imagine yourself performing it.
- List the important aspects of the performance or product. Outline the specific behaviors needed to complete or perform the task.
- Try to limit the number of performance criteria, so that they all can be observed during the pupil's performance. A recommended number of performance criteria to employ is six to twelve.
- If possible, have groups of teachers think through the important criteria included in a task. When teachers in the same grade or those teaching the same objects agree on performance criteria, less confusion exists among students demonstrating the performance.
- Express the performance criteria in terms of observable pupil behaviors or product characteristics. Objectives should be clearly stated in reasonable terms so that they convey the same meaning to different teachers.
- Do not use complex or ambiguous words that cloud the meaning of the performance criteria. Teachers should make sure that words communicate the same meaning to different teachers. Action verbs

such as *compute, demonstrate, show, add,* and *organize* usually communicate the same meanings to different teachers.

• Arrange the performance criteria in the order in which they are likely to be observed. These procedures will save time and will keep pupils focused on tasks.

• Check for existing performance criteria before defining your own. If existing performance criteria are present, teachers should adopt and modify to meet their individual needs.

McTighe (1996) articulates that clearly communicated performance criteria are necessary if tasks are to be properly assessed. Specific and clear criteria must be defined to guide pupils in what is taught and how they are to be assessed. There should be a direct relationship between what is taught and what is assessed.

Provide a Setting to Observe the Performance

The next step in performance assessment is to locate a setting to observe the performance. The type of performance to be observed will greatly depend upon the location and setting. Many performances can be conducted within the classroom. Others will need specific equipment and locations, requiring, for example, structuring a situation where the behavior or task can be performed—where a pupil could demonstrate a scientific experiment or demonstrate the use of some technological device. On the other hand, pupils giving a speech can perform within the classroom, with additional structure. In order to determine a pupil's true performance, multiple performances may need to be conducted.

Scoring the Performance

Some type of system must be used to record and score performances of pupils. Teachers must decide on which techniques they prefer, and both holistic or analytic scoring may be used. Holistic scoring may be used to determine group placement of pupils, to grade performances, or to select pupils for certain groups. When this method is used, teachers are attempting to assess an individual's performance using a single overall score. Analytic scoring is designed to diagnose or assess mastery of each individual performance criterion by using a separate score to rate each performance. In some instances, performance in the arts and athletics may require more than one teacher's observation to determine the performances of pupils. There is a variety of information contained in records for assessing pupils' performances.

ALTERNATIVE ASSESSMENT

Elliott, Ysseldyke, Thurlow, and Erickson (1998) state that alternative assessment is a substitute way of gathering meaningful information on students' learning for those who are unable to take, even with accommodations, the regular assessment. Many children with exceptionalities in the cognitive, social, and physical domains are enrolled in different courses of studies, because their exceptionalities will not permit them to complete the regular curriculum. Typically, these students are working on life skills curricula, which are designed to prepare them for supported or competitive employment, sheltered workshops, group homes, or supervised independent living situations.

Alternative assessment may involve using several formats. Portfolio assessment is commonly used in conducting alternative assessment. Portfolio assessments may include summaries and examples of all of the student's learning, which is checked by the teacher and updated frequently. Other informal types of assessment instruments such as rating scales, checklists, questionnaires, surveys, interviews, and self-report inventories, to name but a few, are used to implement alternative assessment strategies (Witt, Elliott, Daly, Gresham, and Kramer 1998).

Information from Records

Records may provide valuable information relevant to assessing children. Numerous records are at the disposal of educators, such as cumulative records, school databases, portfolios, anecdotal records, and general records not associated with the school. Some systematic procedures need to be developed to assist educators in recording information.

Anecdotal

Anecdotal records provide a written account of the child's behavior. Data from rating scales and checklists may be used to validate narrative statements in anecdotal records. Anecdotal records consume a significant part of a teacher's time to prepare and should be recorded as soon as possible after the behavior occurs. Educators should exercise caution in recording events by separating facts from their interpretations of behaviors. Another caution concerns validity; data should be kept over a period of time to note trends.

Educator's biases, known or unknown, tend to influence the information contained in anecdotal records. There is both observer bias and observed bias. Observer bias may be evident from the recording of invalid behaviors because of some like or dislike of a special characteristic of the observed. Observed bias may result from the fact that the observed may behave differently simply because he/she knows that he or she is being observed.

There are many valuable uses of anecdotal records. To be useful in the instructional program, they should be systematically updated and kept over a period of time and used to strengthen instruction by programming the student's strengths and weaknesses into the curriculum (Rhodes and Nathension-Mejia 1992). The issue of collecting and organizing information in anecdotal records must be carefully considered by the teacher. Some type of systematic plan should be evident, according to Pike and Salend (1995). A three-ring binder that is sectioned off alphabetically by students' last names, a separate notebook, or a card file system may be employed.

Checklists

A checklist may be used to determine whether or not a specific behavior has been observed. If certain behaviors are noted, a *yes* is recorded, if not, a *no* is recorded. Teachers can document the presence or the absence of a behavior. Information derived from checklists can assist the teacher in planning to correct or to delimit any negative behavior in the social, physical, or academic domains by comparing and noting behaviors over a specific time frame. Checklists of characteristics or behaviors arranged in a consistent manner allow the evaluator to check the presence or absence of the characteristics or behaviors over time (Cohen and Spenciner 1998).

Guidelines for developing checklists as advocated by Beaty (1994) and Gronlund and Linn (1990) include the following:

- Checklist items should be brief, yet detailed and easily understood.
- Parallel word construction must be used. The word order, subject, and verb tense should be the same for all items.
- The items should be nonjudgmental.
- The checklist should stress positive behavior.
- Emphasize what the student can do as opposed to what the student cannot do.
- Do not repeat items in different parts of the checklist.
- The items should be representative of students' behavior.
- Arrange the items in the order in which they are expected to appear.
- A procedure must be provided for indicating each behavior as it occurs (e.g., check mark, yes-no, plus or minus sign).

Beatty (1994) sums up the importance of checklists by stating that a checklist can supplement the information obtained from observations, can assist in evaluating a student's behavior, and can be used with one or more students. Checklists have been criticized because they are subjective, lack reliability, and they may not adequately assess the behavior in question.

Rating Scales

Rating scales can provide valuable information used in recording data. Three of the most common types of rating scales are the numerical, graphic, and descriptive scales. In numerical scales a number stands for a point on the scale. Graphic scales require that individuals mark a position on a line divided into sections on the scale. Descriptive rating scales require that an individual choose among different descriptions of actual performance (Wiggins and McTighe 1998; Goodrich 1997). In choosing the type of rating scale to employ, teachers and educators should adhere to the following considerations. Limit the number of rating categories. Large numbers of categories make discrimination less likely. Three to five categories are recommended. Use the same rating system for each performance. Using different rating categories requires the observer to change focus frequently and will decrease accuracy (Airasian 2001).

Rating scales provide data in a structured, sequenced, and standardized way, as well as facilitating data aggregation (Salvia and Ysseldyke 1998). Vaughn, Schumm, and Brick (1998) employed the case study method conducted with three school sites over a four-year period to develop a rating scale. Data from principals, parents, and students provided valuable information used in constructing the rating scale. The scale had eleven major components with several items corresponding with each major component (see Vaughn et al. 1998).

1. Each student's educational needs are considered first.
2. Teacher's skills, knowledge, and attitudes toward inclusion are important.
3. Adequate resources are provided.
4. Parents are involved in the development and implementation of the inclusion model.
5. A continuum of service is maintained.
6. The service delivery model is continually evaluated and altered.
7. Ongoing professional development is encouraged.
8. Philosophy on inclusion is developed at the school level.
9. Curriculum approaches that meet the needs of all students are developed and refined.
10. Roles and responsibilities of the special education teacher and other specialists are outlined.
11. Roles and responsibilities of the general education teacher are defined.

Principal stakeholders reviewed and provided feedback information on the rating scales. These responses were employed in revising the final rating scale. Although the rating scale was developed to assess inclusion programs, there are specific techniques that educators may use for program development, monitoring, and evaluation. Rating scales may provide information for assessing pupils' performances and yield detailed diagnostic information for assessing strengths and weaknesses in several areas of functioning.

Self-Assessment

Although self-assessment is the most underused type of classroom assessment, it has the most flexibility and power as an assessment tool (Marzano 2000). Airasian (2001) supports these views by asserting that self-assessment is central to the development of a higher order, yet it is a cognitive skill that assists in the identification of individual learning goals. Self-assessment can yield valuable information to assist the teacher in understanding how the child feels toward educational issues. When student self-assessments are used by teachers, each individual student rates him- or herself on topics listed in the assessment instrument. The teacher scores the self-assessment and uses data from the instrument to determine whether or not the stated objectives have been achieved. Self-assessment data may come from a variety of sources, such as interviews, journals, logs, questionnaires, checklists, and rating scales.

Construction of instruments used in self-assessment must consider the developmental level of the child in all principal areas such as mental, social, and physical areas. In the case of exceptional children, the type of exceptionality must be carefully considered. In some instances, the teacher will have to assist the child in completing his/her self-assessment (Davison and Pearce 1992).

Rubrics

Rubrics may be defined as clear sets of criteria used to assist teachers and pupils to determine values of an instructional activity. A rubric is a general scoring guide that describes the level at which a pupil performs a task. Scoring rubrics for pupils' outcomes is often an excellent method for assessing pupils' exit outcome proficiencies. Specific scoring rubrics using checklists and rating scales should be designed for each exit outcome proficiency to enable a reliable assessment of the proficiency. Scoring them should include descriptions of the performance or task demonstrated and should reflect an objective assessment of both the pupil's performances and products. There are many common terms that teachers can use to describe scoring levels in rubrics. One commonly used set of adjectives includes *excellent, good, fair, poor,* and another may include *sometimes, seldom, never, always,* and so on. As noted, each of the terms differentiates levels of performance for pupils to demonstrate. These levels of performance describe each criterion under the various levels.

A specific scoring rubric using descriptive criteria should be designed for each exit outcome proficiency that describes the pupils' overall performance on the task being demonstrated. Research findings by Mehrens, Popham, and Ryan (1998); Herbert (1992); Andrade (2000); and Marzano (2000) have all attested to the importance of using rubrics to assess and summarize performances. Collectively their research findings have shown that rubrics may assist students in the following ways, by (1) monitoring their work as well as that of their classmates; (2) understanding the qualities associated with a specific task; (3) developing their critical-thinking skills; and (4) self-assessing their work.

Rubrics can be of value to teachers by assisting them in (1) focusing on teaching and assessing what is essential in pupils' work; (2) communicating their expectations to pupils; and (3) establishing standards and grading procedures with pupils.

Airasian (2001) lists the following steps in preparing and using rubrics:

1. Select a process or product to be taught.
2. State performance criteria for the process or product.
3. Decide on the number of scoring levels for the rubric, usually three to five.
4. State descriptions of performance criteria at the highest level of pupil performance.
5. State descriptions of performance criteria at the remaining scoring levels.
6. Compare each pupil's performance to each scoring level.
7. Select the scoring level that is closest to a pupil's actual performance or product.
8. Grade the pupil.

Portfolio Assessment

A portfolio is a collection of student work that is reviewed against criteria in order to judge an individual student or program. The portfolio does not constitute the assessment; it is simply acceptable work that may or may not be evaluated. Each portfolio should contain an identified assessment purpose; criteria for determining the content of the portfolio; and criteria for assessing the work (Herbert 1992).

The value of using portfolios in assessing the strengths and weaknesses of children has been well documented in the professional literature (Pike and Salend 1995; Salinger 1991; Wolf 1989; Mitchell 1992; O'Neil 1993; Ryan and Miyasaka 1995).

A portfolio may contain a variety of a pupil's work to demonstrate growth and progress toward stated goals. It may contain writing samples, books read, journal notations, book reports, laboratory reports, homework, art work, and computer programs and other technological devices, to name but a few examples. Portfolios may show individual pupil performance, or a variety of pupil performances.

Effective portfolio assessment requires a cooperative effort on the part of teachers, children, and sometimes parents. The assessment should reflect the learning as well as the products of learning. Scoring rubrics should be developed by teachers with input from students. Students should be instructed on how to use the scoring rubrics. Objective information should be reviewed periodically by teachers, children, and parents to update, delete, document, or expand information items selected for inclusion. Items should be directly related to objectives specified in the student's instructional program in order to determine to what degree students have achieved the exit outcomes.

Objectives, scoring procedures, and standards must be established which arc reliable for individuals evaluating portfolios. At least 80 percent agreement should be obtained. Several attempts may be made before 80 percent agreement is achieved using the formula:

$$\frac{\text{Agreement} \times 100}{\text{Agreement Disagreement}}$$

This formula is designed to assess the extent to which different raters agree on what they observe. Two or more raters independently observe the same behavior. Normally, raters should be trained until they reach at least an 80 percent agreement level. Meyer (1992) and Meyer and

Janney (1989) indicate that when scoring portfolios some type of scoring standards and rubrics should be developed. Standards and dimensions of the scoring indicator rubric will assist observers in reaching reliable decisions relevant to agreement on the behaviors. They indicate five standards to consider:

1. Performance of target skills within the context of academic expectations.
2. Appropriate supports that lead to independence.
3. Performance in multiple settings to enhance the generalization of skills.
4. Social relationships that support the development of appropriate social interaction skills and the development of social networks.
5. Age-appropriate performance with opportunities for making choices and decisions.

Depending upon the type of portfolios, some of them may require a great deal of time to score, whereas when they are used to provide descriptive information relevant to a pupil, no scoring may be necessary. Checklists, rating scales, and rubrics are generally used to score multifocused and individual portfolios. Refer to information relevant to the above techniques reported earlier in the chapter.

The listed standards may be used to evaluate students' performances. Specific scoring criteria may be developed for each of the standards. Information from the five standards is clustered and observers give students a single score. The scores are tabulated and a percentage of agreement is computed. The standards and the scoring rubrics may need to be modified for students with disabilities. An alternate portfolio system may need to be instituted with individual rather than group performance expectations or standards (Kearnes, Kleinert, and Kennedy 1999).

Alternate Portfolio

The alternate portfolio may be employed with students for whom the regular assessment program did not provide a meaningful measurement of learning, even with accommodations. Students with disabilities are permitted to demonstrate outcomes in other ways (Kearns, Kleinert, and Kennedy 1999). Some examples may include having an individual with a disability use technology to demonstrate a skill, using various modes of input and output strategies. For example, a child with defective speech asked to classify objects would be permitted to simply point to the objects under the classification. Alternate portfolio assessment, according to Kearns, Kleiner, and Kennedy (1999), should include the following:

1. Evidence of how the student communicates, as indicated in the above example;
2. The student's daily or weekly schedule, based upon strategies used to achieve the standards;
3. A student letter to the reviewer, indicating a rationale for choosing items to report;
4. A resume of work experiences for twelfth graders, specifying the types of real-life vocational experiences completed;
5. A letter from the student's parents or guardian, indicating parental approval and involvement; and
6. Relevant academic entries, which may be items of interest selected by the student to include in the portfolio.

SUMMARY

Performance assessment is increasingly being recognized as an important component of the total evaluation process. Most performance techniques are specific and task-oriented. Teachers have found data from these techniques to be of immense value when integrated with formal techniques in planning and conducting instructional programs. Popham (2002) wrote that there are several evaluative criteria for performance test tasks that teachers can use to assess a student's progress: (1) generalizability, (2) authenticity, (3) multiple foci, (4) teachability, (5) fairness, (6) feasibility, and (7) scoreability (p. 195).

Teachers tend to favor performance techniques over formal assessment because performance assessment does not require a normative sample or standardization procedures. Additionally, assessments are not intended to be complicated, expensive, or time consuming (Wallace, Larsen, and Elksnin 1992). Many performance techniques can be readily adapted and modified to meet the needs of individuals with disabilities.

REFERENCES

Airasian, P. W. 2001. *Classroom assessment: Concepts and applications.* New York: McGraw-Hill.

Andrade, H. G. 2000. Using rubrics to promote thinking and learning. *Educational Leadership* 57 (5), 13–18.

Arter, J. 1999. Teaching about performance assessment. *Educational Measurement: Issues and Practice* 18 (2), 30–44.

Bartz, D., S. Anderson-Robinson, and L. Hillman. 1994. Performance assessment: Make them show what they know. *Principal* 73, 11–14.

Beaty, J. 1994. *Observing development of the young child,* 3rd ed. New York: Macmillan.

Cohen, L. G., and L. J. Spenciner. 1998. *Assessment of children and youth.* New York: Addison-Wesley Longman.

Davison, D. M., and D. L. Pearce. 1992. The influence of writing activities on the mathematics learning of Native American students. *The Journal of Educational Issues of Language Minority Students* 10, 146–57.

Elliott, J., J. Ysseldyke, M. Thurlow, and R. Erickson. 1998. What about assessment and accountability? Practical implications for educators. *Teaching Exceptional Children* 37 (1), 20–27.

Fager, J., B. S. Blake, and J. C. Impara. 1997. Examining teacher educators' knowledge of classroom assessment: A pilot study. Paper presented at the National Council on Measurement in Education National Conference, Chicago.

Goodrich, H. 1997. Understanding rubrics. *Educational Leadership* 54 (4), 14–17.

Gronlund, N. E., and R. L. Linn. 1990. *Measurement and evaluation in teaching.* New York: Macmillan.

Herbert, E. A. 1992. Portfolios invite reflection from both students and staff. *Educational Leadership* 49 (8), 58–61.

Kearns, J. F., H. L. Kleinert, and G. Kennedy. 1999. We need not exclude anyone. *Educational Leadership* 56 (6), 32–38.

Madaus, G. F., and L. M. O'Dwyer. 1999. A short history of performance assessment: Lessons learned. *Phi Delta Kappan* 80 (9), 688–95.

Marzano, R. J. 2000. *Transforming classroom grading*. Alexandria, Va.: Association for Supervision and Curriculum Development.

Marzano, R. J., D. Pickering, and J. McTighe. 1993. *Assessing student outcomes: Performance assessment using the dimensions of learning model*. Alexandria, Va.: Association for Supervision and Curriculum Development.

McTighe, J. 1996. Performance-based assessment in the classroom: A planning framework. In R. Blum and J. Arter, eds., *Student performance in an era of restructuring*. Alexandria, Va.: Association for Supervision and Curriculum Development.

Mehrens, W. A., W. J. Popham, and J. M. Ryan. 1998. How to prepare students for performance assessments. *Educational Measurement: Issues and Practices* 17 (1), 18–22.

Meyer, C. A. 1992. What's the difference between authentic and performance assessment? *Educational Leadership* 49, 39–40.

Meyer, L., J. Eichinger, and J. Downing. 1992. *The program quality indicators (PqI): A checklist of most promising practices in educational programs for students with severe disabilities* (rev. ed.). Syracuse, N.Y.: Syracuse University Division of Special Education and Rehabilitation.

Meyer, L., and R. Janney. 1989. User-friendly measures of meaningful outcomes: Evaluating the behavioral interventions. *Journal of the Association for Persons with Severe Handicaps* 14 (4), 263–70.

Mitchell, R. 1992. *Testing for learning*. New York: Free Press.

O'Neil, J. 1993. *The promise of portfolios*. Alexandria, Va.: Association for Supervision and Curriculum Development.

Pike, K., and S. Salend. 1995. Authentic assessment strategies. *Teaching Exceptional Children* 28 (1), 15–19.

Rhodes, L. K., and S. Nathension-Mejia. 1992. Anecdotal records: A powerful tool for on-going literacy assessment. *The Reading Teachers* 45 (7), 502–509.

Ryan, J., and J. Miyasaka. 1995. Current practices in teaching and assessment: What is driving the change? *NAASP Bulletin* 79, 1–10.

Salinger, T. 1991. *Getting started with alternative assessment methods*. Workshop presented at the New York State Reading Association Conference, Lake Kiamesha, New York.

Salvia, J., and J. E. Ysseldyke. 1998. *Assessment*. Boston: Houghton-Mifflin.

Stiggins, R. J. 1997. *Student-centered classroom assessment*. Columbus, Ohio: Prentice-Hall.

Vaughn, S., J. S. Schumm, and J. B. Brick. 1998. Using a rating scale to design and evaluate inclusion programs. *Teaching Exceptional Children* 30 (4), 41–45.

Wallace, G., S. C. Larsen, and L. K. Elksnin. 1992. *Educational assessment of learning problems: Testing for teaching.* Boston: Allyn and Bacon.

Wiggins, G. 1992. Creating tests worth taking. *Educational Leadership* 44 (8), 26–33.

Wiggins, G., and J. McTighe. 1998. *Understanding by design.* Alexandria, Va.: Association for Supervision and Curriculum Development.

Witt, J. C., S. N. Elliott, E. J. Daly III, F. M. Gresham, and J. J. Kramer. 1998. *Assessment of at-risk and special needs children.* New York: McGraw-Hill.

Wolf, D. P. 1989. Portfolio assessment sampling student work. *Educational Leadership* 46 (7), 35–39.

CHAPTER 6

Assessing Learning Styles

Children receive and order information differently and through a variety of dimensions and channels. Mason and Egel (1995) imply that teachers frequently find it difficult to assess an individual's learning style preference. Making sense out of the world is a very real and active process. During early childhood, children master complex tasks according to their own schedules without formal training or intervention. The structured environment of the school appears to impede the personal learning styles of many exceptional individuals. Pupils enter school with a wide range of learning abilities, interests, motivations, personalities, attitudes, cultural orientations, and social status. The teacher must consider all of those traits in planning an instructional program (O'Brien 1989; Taylor 2001; Hilliard 1989).

COGNITIVE DIMENSION

The cognitive dimension of learning refers to the different ways that children mentally perceive and order information and ideas. Some children are abstract learners, others are concrete learners. Various instructional approaches must be developed for each learning style.

AFFECTIVE DIMENSION

Affective dimension refers to how students' personality traits—both social and emotional—affect their learning. This dimension involves feelings, attitudes, interests, values, and emotions. Affective characteristics include personality, emotional state, motivation, self-esteem, and trust-worthiness (Airasian 2001). Teachers informally observe these traits to determine how pupils react in the classroom as well as how these traits may affect learning. These dimensions tend to indicate that learning styles are functions of both nature and nurture and can have a positive or negative impact upon personality development (Taylor 1998).

PHYSIOLOGICAL DIMENSION

The physiological dimension of learning involves the interaction of the senses and the environment. There are several channels under the physiological dimension: visual, auditory, tactile/kinesthetic, and a mixed combination of five senses. Does the student learn bet-ter through auditory, visual, or tactile/kinesthetic means? And how is he or she affected by such factors as light, temperature, and room design?

PSYCHOLOGICAL DIMENSION

The psychological dimension involves the students' inner strengths and individuality. Flexibility in working in the context of many styles within the classroom can offer the teacher the opportunity to reach a va-riety of children with different learning styles. The benefits of flexibil-ity in teaching are immeasurable (Taylor 1998).

Research findings by Guild (1994) strongly suggest that the domi-nant qualities of a learner's style are unchangeable. Teachers can assist learners by being flexible in their teaching and recognize the impact of learning styles on pupils' learning. A teacher who is aware of his or her own most comfortable teaching style as well as the style most com-fortable for the pupil can best promote learning.

EVALUATING LEARNING STYLES

Pupils learn through a variety of sensory channels and have individual patterns of sensory strengths and weaknesses. Teachers should capital-ize on this and use the learning styles of pupils in their academic programs. Exceptional individuals go through the same general development sequence; however, due to developmental problems, some progress at a slower rate. Several factors should be considered in characterizing a pupil's learning style:

1. The speed at which a pupil learns is an important aspect to consider. A pupil's learning rate is not as obvious as it may appear. Frequently, a learner's characteristics interfere with his or her natural learning rate. Although the learning rate is more observable than other characteristics, it does not necessarily relate to the quality of a learner's performance. Therefore, it is of prime importance for the teacher to know as much as possible about all of a learner's characteristics.

2. The techniques the pupil uses to organize materials he or she plans to learn is significant. Some individuals organize information to be learned by remembering the broad ideas. These broad ideas then trigger details in the pupil's memory. This method of proceeding from the general to the specific is referred to as the deductive style of organization. This principle may be applied in many situations. Other pupils prefer to remember the smaller components which then remind them of the broader concept, an inductive style of organization. In utilizing inductive organization, the pupil may look at several items or objectives, form specific characteristics, and develop general principles or concepts. Knowing an exceptional individual's style of organization can assist the teacher to effectively guide the learning process by presenting materials as close as possible to the student's preferred style of organization (Mason and Egel 1995).

3. The pupil's need for reinforcement in the learning situation should be considered. All learners need some structure and reinforcement to their learning. This process may be facilitated through a pupil's preferred channels of input and output.

4. Input involves using the five sensory channels—auditory, tactile, kinesthetic, olfactory, and gustatory. These stimuli are transmitted to the brain. In the brain, the sensory stimuli are organized into cognitive patterns referred to as perception. The input through

which a student most readily processes stimuli is referred to as his or her preferred modality.

5. Output may be expressed verbally or nonverbally. Verbal output uses the fine motor activity of the speech mechanism to express oral language. Nonverbal output uses both fine and gross motor activities. Fine motor skills may include gesture and demonstration. Pupils usually prefer to express themselves through one of these outputs.

6. A pupil's preferred model of input is not necessarily his or her strongest acuity channel. Sometimes a pupil will transfer information received through one channel into another in which he or she is more comfortable. This process is called intermodal transfer. Failure to perform this task effectively may impede learning (Taylor 2001).

DIVERSE LEARNING STYLES

The learning styles and patterns of some pupils almost assure rewarding educational achievement for the successful completion of tasks. This is, unfortunately, not true for many exceptional individuals. The differences in learning styles can cause interferences with the exceptional individual's achievement. The educational environment of exceptional individuals is a critical factor. The early identification, assessment, and management of an exceptional individual's learning-style differences by the teacher can prevent more serious learning problems from occurring.

Children display diverse skills in learning. This necessitates proven knowledge as well as sound theories on the teacher's part for successful teaching. Some educators who are interested in the development of children often lack the necessary understanding of how children learn, what they are interested in, and how to put these two together. Due to wide individual differences among exceptional individuals, instructional techniques must vary. Individuals with exceptionalities need special attention; their teachers need special orientation to meet their special needs. The teacher must know what can be expected of students and then try to adapt the activities to their capabilities.

It has been voiced that no activity provides a greater variety of opportunities for learning than creative dramatics. In creative dramatics work children are given specific objectives and values, and exercises in pantomime, improvisation, and play structure, and they follow the procedures involved in preparing a play. As more is discovered about learning and in particular the variety of ways certain exceptional individuals learn, we are finding that creative dramatics add immeasurable knowledge to the development of a theoretical construct for various types of learning styles. Equally important, these techniques may lead to the discovery of different learning styles at various developmental levels (Taylor 1998).

In spite of the paucity of research studies in the area of learning styles, it is generally recognized that individuals learn through a variety of sensory channels and have individual patterns of sensory strengths and weaknesses. Some exceptional individuals seem to have adequate sensory acuity but are unable to utilize their sensory channels effectively. It then becomes of tantamount importance to discover techniques for assessing the individual's sensory strengths and weaknesses, and to identify ways that materials can be presented to capitalize on these sensory strengths and weaknesses. This does not necessarily mean that materials should be presented to the pupil via his or her preferred style, but it would mean that credit be given for his or her strength (e.g., hearing) while he or she worked to overcome other weaknesses (e.g., vision). Basic to the concept of learning styles is the recognition that the teacher initiate and sustain the learning process.

CHARACTERIZING LEARNING STYLES

A major concern of all education is to assist individuals in realizing their full learning potentialities. Educational services should be designed to take into account individual learning behavior and style. To be able to accomplish this task it is required that we know something about the pupil as a learner. The Maryland State Department of Education's Division of Instructional Television (1973) has listed several ways to characterize a pupil's learning style, by observing (1) the speed at which a pupil learns, (2) the techniques the pupil uses to organize materials he or she hopes to learn, (3) the pupil's need for reinforcement and structure in the learning situation, (4) the channels of input through which the pupil's mind proceeds, and (5) the channels of output through which the pupil best shows how much he or she has learned.

The speed with which a pupil learns is important for individualizing instruction. Observations of the learner's characteristics will facilitate planning for his or her individual needs. A keen observer should be cognizant of the various ways an individual organizes materials. Some children learn best by proceeding from general to specific details, others from specific to general details. Knowing a pupil's style of organization can assist the teacher in individualizing his or her instruction. All learners need some structure and reinforcement in their learning. Pupils who have had successful experiences tend to repeat them. Proceeding from simple to complex, or from known to unknown principles provides opportunities for successful experiences for children.

The senses provide the only contact that any individual has with his or her environment. Sensory stimulations are received through the five sensory channels: auditory, visual, tactile, olfactory, and gustatory. These stimuli are organized into cognitive patterns called perceptions. The input channel through which the person most readily processes stimuli is referred to as his or her preferred modality. The one through which he or she processes stimuli less readily is the weaker modality. Similar differences are also apparent in output, which may be expressed verbally or nonverbally. Individuals usually prefer to express themselves through one of these channels.

A pupil's preferred mode of input is not necessarily related to his or her strongest acuity channel. Individuals with impaired vision may still process the vision stimuli they receive more efficiently than they do auditory stimuli. Sometimes a pupil will transfer information received through one channel into another with which he or she is more comfortable. This process is called intermodal transfer. An example of intermodal transfer might be the pupil who whispers each word as he or she reads it. The pupil is attempting to convert the visual stimuli (the printed word) into auditory stimuli (the whispering). Pupils differ in their ability to perform the intermodal transfer. For many exceptional individuals, failure to perform the intermodal transfer may hamper learning.

LEARNING STYLES VERSUS INSTRUCTIONAL STRATEGIES

Many exceptional individuals might be using their preferred channels of input, which could be their weakest modality. Therefore, it is essential that the pupil's preferred mode of input and output be assessed. A variety of formal or informal techniques may be employed. Differentiation of instructional techniques based on assessment will improve the pupil's efficiency as a learner.

Tables 6.1, 6.2, and 6.3 have been prepared to provide some possible behaviors, assessment techniques, and instructional procedures to assist the teacher working with exceptional individuals. These tables describe three basic modalities: auditory, visual, and tactile kinesthetic. The olfactory and the gustatory modalities are not included in the tables because they involve detailed medical and psychological insights that are outside the realm of education. Specific behaviors that are characteristics for auditory, visual, and tactile kinesthetic modalities are given, with suggestions for possible techniques that might be employed.

It appears to be psychologically sound that exceptional individuals should be introduced to new tasks through their strongest input channels and should review tasks presented to the weak channels. The concept of learning styles holds great promise for facilitating the achievement of exceptional individuals, and we hope that more will be discovered about sensory acuity and the inability of some individuals to use their sense modalities effectively. Some children are concrete learners, others are abstract learners, others focus on global aspects of the problem, and some focus on specific points. Since schools traditionally give more weight to analytical approaches than to holistic approaches, the teacher who does not manifest analytical habits is at a decided disadvantage (Hilliard 1989).

Table 6.1. The Auditory Modality*

Possible Behaviors Pupil Who Is Strong Auditorily MAY		Possible Techniques The Teacher May Utilize:		
Show the Following Strengths	Show the Following Weaknesses	Formal Assessment Techniques	Informal Assessment Techniques	Instructional Techniques
Follow oral instructions very easily.	Lose place in visual activities.	Present statement verbally; ask pupil to repeat.	Observe pupil reading with the use of finger or pencil as a marker.	Reading: stress phonetic analysis, avoid emphasis on sight vocabulary or fast reading. Allow pupils to use markers, fingers, etc., to keep their place.
Do well in tasks sequencing phonetic analysis.	Read word by word.	Tap auditory pattern beyond pupil's point of vision. Ask pupil to repeat pattern.	Observe whether pupil whispers or barely produces sounds to correspond to his/her reading task.	
Appear brighter than tests show him/her to be.	Reverse words when reading.			Arithmetic: Provide audio tapes of story problems. verbally explain arithmetic processes as well as demonstrate.
Sequence speech sounds with facility.	Make visual discrimination errors.	Provide pupil with several words in rhyming family. Ask pupil to add more.	Observe pupil who has difficulty following purely visual directions.	
Perform well verbally.	Have difficulty with written work; poor motor skill.	Present pupil with sounds produced out of his/her field of vision. Ask him/her if they are the same or different.		Spelling: Build on syllabication skills; utilize sound clues.
	Have difficulty copying from the chalkboard.			Generally: Utilize work sheets with large unhampered areas. Use lined wide-spaced paper. Allow for verbal rather than written responses.

*Reprinted with permission of the Maryland State Department of Education, Division of Instructional Television.

Table 6.2. The Visual Modality*

Possible Behaviors Pupil Who Is Strong Visually MAY		Formal Assessment Techniques	Informal Assessment Techniques	Possible Techniques The Teacher May Utilize: Instructional Techniques
Show the Following Strengths	Show the Following Weaknesses			
Possess good sight vocabulary.	Have difficulty with oral directions.	Give lists of words that sound alike. Ask pupil to indicate if they are the same or different.	Observe pupil in tasks requiring sound discrimination, i.e., rhyming, sound blending.	Reading: Avoid phonetic emphasis; stress sight vocabulary, configuration, clues, context clues.
Demonstrate rapid reading skills.	Ask, "what are we supposed to do" immediately after oral instructions are given.	Ask pupil to follow specific instructions. Begin with one direction and continue with multiple instructions.	Observe pupil's sight vocabulary skills. Pupil should exhibit good sight vocabulary skills.	Arithmetic: Show examples of arithmetic function.
Skim reading materials.	Appear confused with great deal of auditory stimuli.	Show pupil visually similar pictures. Ask him/her to indicate whether they are the same or different.	Observe to determine if the pupil performs better when he/she can see the stimulus.	Spelling: Avoid phonetic analysis; stress structural clues, configuration clues.
Read well from picture clues.	Have difficulty discriminating between words with similar sounds.	Show pupil a visual pattern, i.e., block design or pegboard. Ask pupil to duplicate.		Generally: Allow a pupil with strong auditory skills to act as another child's partner. Allow for written rather than verbal responses.
Follow visual diagrams and other visual instructions well.				
Score well on group tests.				
Perform nonverbal tasks well.				

*Reprinted with permission of the Maryland State Department of Education, Division of Instructional Television.

Table 6.3. The Tactile Kinesthetic Modality*

| Possible Behaviors | | Possible Techniques The Teacher May Utilize: | | |
| Pupil Who Is Strong Tactile Kinesthetically MAY | | | | |
Show the Following Strengths	Show the Following Weaknesses	Formal Assessment Techniques	Informal Assessment Techniques	Instructional Techniques
Exhibit good fine and gross motor balance.	Depends on the "guiding" modality or preferred modality since tactile kinesthetic is usually a secondary modality. Weaknesses may be in either the visual or auditory mode.	Ask pupil to walk balance beam or along painted line.	Observe pupil in athletic tasks.	Reading: Stress the shape and structure of the word; use configuration clues, sandpaper letters, have pupil trace the letters and/or words
Exhibit good rhythmic movements.		Set up obstacle course involving gross motor manipulation.	Observe pupil maneuvering in classroom space.	Arithmetic: Utilize objects in performing the arithmetic functions, provide buttons, packages of sticks, etc.
Demonstrate neat handwriting skills.		Have pupil cut along straight, angled, and curved lines.	Observe pupil's spacing of written work on a paper.	
Demonstrate good cutting skills.		Ask child to color find areas.	Observe pupil's selection of activities during free play, i.e., does he/she select puzzles or blocks as opposed to records or picture books.	Spelling: Have pupil write the word in large movements, i.e., air, on chalkboard, on newsprint, utilize manipulative letters to spell the word. Call pupil's attention to the feel of the word. Have pupil write word in cursive to get feel of the whole word by flowing motion.
Manipulate puzzles and other materials well.				
Identify and match objects				

*Reprinted with permission of the Maryland State Department of Education, Division of Instructional Television.

Assessment of the pupil's preferred model of input and output may be conducted through formal and informal techniques. A commonly used instrument is "The Learning Channel Preference Checklist." This checklist is divided into three major sections as outlined.

THE LEARNING CHANNEL PREFERENCE CHECKLIST

The learning channel preference checklist is designed for assessing learning styles. Teachers can administer this checklist and follow up with interpretive discussions. Some modification and adaptation will be needed for exceptional individuals depending upon their disabilities.

Students are asked to rank each statement in the checklist as it relates to them. There are no right or wrong answers. Students rate each item as often (3), sometimes (2), and never (1), on three broad categories: visual, auditory, and haptic (touch). The highest score indicates a preferred learning style in one of the aforementioned categories.

Auditory Learning Style

This is the least developed learning channel for most children, including exceptional individuals. Most children using the checklist do not report this channel as their strongest.

Visual Learning Style

Many children learn best when they can see information. High scores in this area on the checklist denote that the child prefers textbooks over lectures and relies on lists, graphs, charts, pictures, and taking notes. Significantly, more children rate this area higher than the auditory channel.

Haptic Learning Style

Haptic, or tactile kinesthetic, is the most common learning channel reported by children. In essence, most children prefer this style. Haptic students show a cluster of right-brained characteristics. They learn best from experimenting rather than from lectures and textbooks.

The combined scores in the three areas on the checklist usually range from 10 to 30. Usually two learning channels will be closely rated. Scores in the high 20s indicate that the student has satisfactorily developed all three channels and is able to use the modality that best fits the task. Scores below 20 indicate that the student has not yet developed a strong learning channel preference.

Usually students scoring in the 20s have great difficulty with school because they do not have a clearly defined method for processing information. These students should be treated as haptic learners because the haptic style is much easier to develop than the others.

According to O'Brien (1989) the checklist will indicate areas of strengths and weaknesses in sensory acuity. Teachers can then adapt or modify the instructional program to include activities to support the strongest modality. Information from the checklist should be shared with the student. O'Brien (1989, p. 87) states that, "All students benefit from knowing their learning styles, as well as how to use and manipulate them in the learning process."

Another well-known instrument for assessing learning styles is the Myers-Briggs Type Indicator. Learning styles are assessed from basic perceptual and judging traits. The Swassing-Barbe Modality Index assesses auditory, visual, and tactile activity by asking individuals to repeat patterns using the above modalities. Results also show differences in cognitive strengths, such as holistic and global learning in contrast to analytical (Guild 1994).

These tests are culture and language specific. Individuals respond to and interpret self-reporting instruments through their cultural experiences. These responses may be in conflict with established norms and yield conflicting results. Consequently, caution is needed when interpreting results, especially from individuals with disabilities (Taylor 1998).

SUMMARY

Research findings by Baruth and Manning (1992) and Guild (1994) clearly demonstrate the relationship of culture to learning style. Generally, they find that individuals from certain cultures have a preference for specific learning styles and this preference may affect classroom performance. Teachers of individuals with disabilities must recognize that pupils may have a favored learning style that is not in concert with the teacher's styles of instructing. Students learn more effectively when teachers recognize and take into consideration the preferenced learning styles of pupils (Hilliard 1989).

REFERENCES

Airasian, P. W. 2001. *Classroom assessment: Concepts and applications*. New York: McGraw-Hill.

Baruth, L. G., and M. L. Manning. 1992. *Multicultural education of children and adolescents*. Boston: Allyn and Bacon.

Guild, P. 1994. The cultural learning style connection. *Educational Leadership* 51, 16–21.

Hilliard, A. G. 1989. Teachers and culture styles in a pluralistic society. *NEA Today* 7, 65–69.

Maryland State Department of Education. 1973. *Assessing learning styles of exceptional individuals*. Baltimore, Md.: Division of Instructional Television.

Mason, E., and A. L. Egel. 1995. What does Amy like?: Using a mini-reinforcer in instructional activities. *Teaching Exceptional Children* 28, 42–45.

O'Brien, L. 1989. Learning styles: Make the student aware. *NASSP Bulletin*, October, 85–89.

Taylor, G. R. 1998. *Curriculum strategies for teaching social skills to the disabled: Dealing with inappropriate behaviors*. Springfield, Ill.: Charles C. Thomas.

———. 2001. *Educational interventions and services for children with exceptionalities: Strategies and perspectives*. Springfield, Ill.: Charles C. Thomas.

CHAPTER 7

Analyzing and Evaluating Informal Assessment Data

Field statistics is generally broken down into two major areas: descriptive statistics and inferential statistics. The functions of the two differ. Descriptive statistics is used to describe quantitatively how a particular characteristic is distributed among a group of people. Inferential statistics is used to determine how likely it is that characteristics exhibited by a sample of people are an accurate description of those characteristics exhibited by the population of people from which the sample was drawn. Since most professional research literature consists of quantitative material, teachers who have had little experience reading published statistical studies often have difficulty understanding what was read. Teachers need to be informed about appropriate statistics to use to evaluate informal assessment techniques. In the opinion of the author, a working knowledge of descriptive statistics is needed to show strengths and weaknesses of pupils. It is the opinion of the author that an understanding of descriptive statistics is needed for teachers to evaluate the results of informal assessment. The role of inferential statistics is beyond the scope of this chapter. The reader is referred to any basic book in statistics.

DESCRIPTIVE STATISTICS

Teachers may use descriptive statistics when evaluating students, reporting findings, and presenting data from informal assessments. For example, in a situation where a teacher is using observational data to assess behavioral changes in pupils, he or she may compare changes in behavior over a period of time. Preobservational data will be compared with past observational data. A variety of descriptive statistics may be used such as percentiles, mean scores, median scores, and computing the range. These measures yield numerical data and are frequently called quantitative measures. Any basic statistics book may be consulted concerning the method.

Teachers should have some way of evaluating numerical data yielded from informal assessments. Many of the instruments discussed in chapters 3 and 11 can be evaluated using descriptive statistics. Data from informal assessment instruments can also be compared with formal assessment instruments to note strengths and weaknesses demonstrated by children. Results from these assessments can also be used to report progress to parents and to justify to parents grades assigned.

MEASURE OF CENTRAL TENDENCY

Since the concept of average is a descriptive statistic, teachers need to know that there are three kinds of averages used in statistics. They are the mean, the median, and the mode. Most statisticians refer to the average by using the term *measure of central tendency*. The mean, the median, and the mode are all measures of central tendency (Hinkle, Wiersma, and Jurs 1994; Dowdy and Wearden 1991; Gravetter and Wallnau 1996).

The Mean

The mean is the most frequently and commonly used measure of central tendency in scientific research. It is the arithmetic average of a set of scores and is calculated by summing all data values and dividing them by the number of points summed. The formula for the mean is:

$$x = \Sigma X / N$$

where:

μ = the population
Σ = to add
X = data values
N = number of items in a population

When performing a descriptive function, the statistician utilizes rules and procedures for presenting data in a more usable form where

x = the sample mean
X = the data value
N = the number of items in a sample

The Median and the Mode

The median (Md) divides a frequency distribution into two equal parts so that the number of scores below the median equals the number of scores above the median. The mode (Mo) is the score that occurs with the greatest frequency. The median is a positional average and its value is influenced only by the value of the central observations; extreme values do not greatly influence the value of the median. Therefore, when extreme values are evident, the median generally yields a more representative measure than does the mean (Taylor 2000). The mode assumes that the value that occurs more frequently than any other is most typical. The mode has limited use, especially for quantitative data. Often a data set will not contain any repeated values, therefore, in those cases no mode exists.

VARIABILITY

Where variability is concerned, the more similar the scores, the less variability. The amount of variability differs from group to group as shown in table 7.1.

Table 7.1.   Sample of Scores for Three Groups of Children (n = 15)

	Group A	Group B	Group C
	80	76	85
	80	72	80
	80	80	75
	80	70	70
	80	72	80
Sum	400	370	390
Mean	80	74	78
Median	80	72	80
Mode	80	73	80

In table 7.1, we can see that there is no variability at all in the set of scores of Group A because all the children in that group received the same exact score on their tests. The children in Group B show some variability within the distribution, as do the children in Group C. Although the scores in Group C were relatively higher than those in Group B, there is similar variability in the two groups.

Teachers often find nothing unusual in expressing an average in the form of some number. The concept of average is familiar to most teachers, but because they are not used to thinking of variability in quantitative terms, teachers sometimes find it difficult to grasp the conceptual meaning of measures of variability.

THE RANGE

The range (R) considers only the extreme values within a data set. The range of a set of scores is defined by the lowest (L) and the highest (H) score in the set:

$$R = H - L$$

For example, in table 7.1, you can see that Group A has a range that goes from 80 to 80. Using the formula for the range, teachers can calculate the range for Group A and find that it is "0" (zero). Group B has a range that goes from 70 to 80 and Group C has a range that goes from 70 to 85. This measure of dispersion is meaningful but is of little use because of its instability, particularly when it is based on a small sample. If there is one extreme score in a distribution, the dispersion of scores will appear to be large when in fact the removal of that score may reveal an otherwise compressed or compact distribution.

VARIABILITY ABOUT THE MEAN

Of greater interest in descriptive statistics are measures of variability that describe how a set of scores is distributed about the mean. Such measures take into account the variability of all scores in a set and distinguish between the amounts of variability exhibited by different group's scores. In other words, these measures can inform us that in table 7.1, the scores of Group B are distributed relatively closely around Group B's mean, but that the scores of Group C are distributed relatively more widely around Group C's mean.

The average amount by which each score in Group C differs from its mean is larger than the average amount by which each score in Group B differs from its mean. To make certain that this statement is true, one must determine the average amount by which each score differs from its respective group mean. The best way to check this is to subtract the group's mean from each score, as shown in table 7.2.

THE SUM OF THE DIFFERENCES EQUALS ZERO

When we examine table 7.2, we can see that the differences in each group were added together and then divided by the number of differences to determine the average. However, when we add up the differences for both groups, the sum turns out to be zero. If we divide zero by five, which is the number of differences in each group, we get zero. If you subtract the mean of the set from each number in the set and add up the differences, the sum is always zero. It is at this point that many teachers may begin to have difficulty with statistics. Teachers often are not told that subtracting the mean from each score in a set and adding up the differences always yields a product of zero.

By knowing this fact, it should be easier for teachers to grasp conceptually why the computation of variability is not as straightforward as it would appear to be. Take notice in table 7.2 that the differences between scores and their respective means add up to zero because the negative differences cancel out the positive differences. The sum inevitably must be zero.

Table 7.2   Differences Between Scores and their Respective Means for Groups B and C

Group B	Difference	Group C	Difference
Scores	Score-Mean	Scores	Score-Mean
80	$80-74 = 6$	85	$85-78 = 7$
76	$76-74 = 2$	80	$80-78 = 2$
72	$72-74 = -2$	80	$80-78 = 2$
72	$72-74 = -2$	75	$75-78 = -3$
70	$70-74 = -4$	70	$70-78 = -8$
****	Sum of Differences = 0	****	Sum of Differences = 0

THE SUM OF SQUARES AND VARIANCE

One way to eliminate the dilemma is to get rid of the negative differences. There are a number of possible ways to eliminate negative differences but statisticians do it by squaring the difference of the scores produced. Multiplying one negative number by another negative number yields a positive number. If we take the different scores shown in table 7.2 for Groups B and C and square them, you can see the results in table 7.3. We do this by calculating the Sum of Squares (SS):

$$SS = \Sigma X^2 - (\Sigma X)^2 N$$

or

$$SS = \Sigma (X - M)^2$$

The Variance is calculated as follows:

$$S)^2 = SS/(N-1)$$

or

$$\Sigma (X - M)^2 / N$$

where S = variance. In other words, the arithmetic means is subtracted from each score; the differences are then squared, summed, and divided by the total number of observations. The variance expresses the average dispersion in the distribution of scores not in the original units of measurement but in squared units.

Table 7.3.   Squares of Difference Scores of Group B and C

Group B Difference	Group B Difference²	Group C Difference	Group C Difference²
Score-Mean	Score-Mean²	Score-Mean	Score-Mean²
6	36	7	49
2	4	2	4
−2	+4	−3	+9
−2	+4	−3	+9
−4	+16	−8	+64
****	Sum of Squares = 64	****	Sum of Squares = 135

Table 7.3 reveals that the sum of squares for Group B is 64 and for Group C is 135. If we divide the sum of squares by the number of scores, the end result is called the variance. The variance for Group B is 64 / 5 = 12.8 and the variance for Group C is 135 / 5 = 27. The variance shows how much the average squared difference between each score and the mean score is.

THE STANDARD DEVIATION

Once the sum of squares has been calculated, the next step to consider in the order of statistical operations is the calculation of the standard deviation. The formula for this is as follows:

$$SD = \Sigma(X - M)^2/N$$

or

$$S = S^2$$

The standard deviation is the most common measure of validity used in statistics (Bogdan and Biklen 1982). It is the square root of the average squared difference between each score and the mean score. This means that the standard deviation reveals a close approximation of the average amount by which each score differs from the group's mean; basically, how far apart scores deviate from the mean (Blaisdell 1993; Dowdy and Wearden 1991; Bruning and Kintz 1987).

Since the standard deviation is the square root of the variance, the standard deviation for Group B is 3.57 (the square root of 12.8) and the standard deviation for Group C is 5.09 (the square root of 27). This means that the average amount by which each score in Group B differs from Group B's mean is 3.57, and the average amount by which each score in Group C differs from Group C's mean is approximately 5.09. The larger the standard deviation (SD), the greater the amount of variability (Elmore and Woehlke 1997). The standard deviation of 5.09 in Group C indicates more variability than the standard deviation of 3.57 of Group B.

The most important thing that teachers should remember about the concept of standard deviation is that a standard deviation approximates the amount by which each score in a group differs from the group's mean score. Jacob (1987) said "because the sum of the differences between each score and the mean always equals zero, to calculate the standard deviation it is first necessary to square the differences to eliminate the negative differences and then take the square root to undo the squaring process."

When using descriptive statistics to describe how test scores are distributed among Groups A, B, and C, you should indicate that Group B has a mean (M) of 74 and a standard deviation (SD) of 3.57. Likewise, you should indicate that Group C has a mean (M) of 78 and a standard deviation (SD) of 5.09. The mean (M) for Group A is 80 and has a standard deviation (SD) of "0" (zero). This information indicates that although both groups have means that are close numerically (74 and 78, respectively), the scores in Group C have more variability. There may be occasions when some groups may have different means but have the same standard deviation. In such cases, this indicates that one group, on the average, performs at a higher level than the other groups, but the amount of variability at that level within each group is the same.

Finally, the two groups may have both different means and different standard deviations. According to Campbell and Stanley (1963, p. 298), consider the following examples:

> One group of students achieves a mean score of 72 points on an informal spelling test and another group achieves a mean of 80. It is clear that the group with a mean of 80 performed better than the other group. Suppose it turns out that on the same test, one group has a standard deviation of 3 and the other a standard deviation of 10. It should be clear that there is more variability in the scores of the group with the standard deviation of 10 than in the group with the standard deviation of 3.

In this example it was not stated which group had which mean or which standard deviation. The group with the lower mean might have either a lower or a higher standard deviation than the group with the higher mean. There is not a consistent relationship between the magnitude of a mean and the magnitude of a standard deviation (Cook and Campbell 1979).

FREQUENCY DISTRIBUTIONS

Let's examine the following hypothetical situation. Your supervisor has given you the responsibility of conducting a ninety-day feasibility study regarding perceptions of fifth grade students toward the use of a new computerized program in reading. A Likert-type scale was developed to assess perceptions. Data were analyzed using descriptive methods previously cited. First a frequency distribution table was constructed, listing the scores from the scale. The frequency distribution allows teachers to make certain assumptions for the data gathered. In the example given, the frequency distribution will allow teachers to assume or not assume that pupils will or will not have positive perceptions toward the use of the computerized program. Means and median graphs and charts may then be computed and constructed to support the teacher's assumptions. In some cases it may become necessary to group some scores into what is referred to as class intervals and then obtain a frequency distribution of grouped scores.

GROUPED FREQUENCY DISTRIBUTION

Grouping into class intervals involves "collapsing the scale" and assigning scores to mutually exclusive and exhaustive classes where the classes are defined in terms of grouping intervals used. The reasons for grouping are threefold:

1. It is uneconomical and unwieldly to deal with a large number of cases spread out over many scores.
2. Some scores have low frequency counts so we are not justified in maintaining these scores as separate entities.
3. Categories provide a concise and meaningful summary of the data.

The following steps may be used to arrange data into class intervals:

Step 1 Find the difference between the highest and lowest scores contained in the original data. Add 1 to obtain the total number of scores or potential scores.

Step 2   Divide 75 by 15, the number of class intervals, to obtain the number of scores or potential scores in each class interval. If the resulting value is not a whole number, round to the nearest odd number so a whole number will be at the middle of the class interval.

Step 3   Take the lowest score in the original data as the minimum value in the lowest class interval. Add this to −1 to obtain the maximum score of the lowest class interval.

Step 4   The next highest class interval begins at the integer following the maximum score of the lower class interval. Follow the same procedures as in Step 3 to obtain the maximum score of the second class interval. Follow these procedures for each successive higher class interval until all scores are included in their appropriate class intervals.

Step 5   Assign each score to the class interval within which it is included.

As indicated, teachers may use class interval data to compute measures of central tendency, percentiles, the range, and to locate scores that fall in the first, second, and third quartiles. Results may be used to (1) report students' progress to parents, (2) assign grades, (3) group children for instruction, and (4) make changes in the instructional program, to name some of the major uses of data.

SUMMARY

In describing data from informal instruments it is not enough for teachers to know the average point around a set of scores. They must also know how spread out or how dispersed the scores are. Additionally, teachers will need an indicator of variability, such as the range and the standard deviation. By using descriptive statistics, teachers can analyze the effectiveness of their instruction, as well as determine the strengths and weaknesses of pupils in areas of the curriculum. Expert assistance may be needed by teachers to conduct some of the statistical treatment under descriptive statistics. Additionally, there are available statistical books that teachers may also consult.

REFERENCES

Blaisdell, E. A. 1993. *Statistics in practice*. New York: Sanders College Publishing Company.

Bogdan, R. C., and S. K. Biklen. 1982. *Qualitative research for education: An introduction to theory and methods.* Boston: Allyn and Bacon.

Bruning, J. L., and B. L. Kintz. 1987. *Computational handbook of statistics,* 3rd ed. Glenview, Ill.: Scott Foresman.

Campbell, D. T., and J. C. Stanley. 1963. *Experimental and quasi-experimental design for research*. Chicago: Rand McNally.

Cook, T. D., and D. T. Campbell. 1979. *Quasi-experimentation*. Chicago: Rand McNally.

Dowdy, S., and S. Wearden. 1991. *Statistics for research,* 2nd ed. New York: John Wiley and Sons.

Elmore, P. B., and P. L. Woehlke. 1997. *Basic statistics*. New York: Longman.

Gravetter, F. J., and L. B. Wallnau. 1996. *Statistics for the behavioral sciences* New York: West Publishing Company.

Hinkle, D. E., W. Wiersma, and S. G. Jurs. 1994. *Applied statistics for the behavioral sciences*. Boston: Houghton-Mifflin Company.

Jacob, E. 1987. Qualitative research traditions: A review. *Review of Educational Research* 57, 1–50.

Taylor, G. R. 2000. *Integrating quantitative and qualitative methods in research*. Lanham, Md.: University Press of America.

CHAPTER 8

Communicating Assessment Data to Parents

Due to the importance of testing data and information used both for administrative and legal purposes, special education administrators must establish and monitor procedures regarding their use, access, care, and storage. All school districts must maintain student testing data, including informal tests and files as required by state and federal regulations (Podemski, Marsh II, Smith, and Price 1995). According to the Federal Register (1977), an educational accessible record is defined by the Department of Health, Education, and Welfare as being directly related to a student and maintained by an educational agency. Accessible records include test results and any assessment information used for decision making. Information kept by an individual for private use is not regarded as an accessible record.

Podemski, Marsh II, Smith, and Price (1995) sum up the importance of special education administrators safeguarding records. They indicate that in recent years, access to students' records has become a somewhat sensitive issue among parents as well as administrators. School administrators have reported instances of teachers misplacing records and sharing confidential data in inappropriate situations. As a result of litigation regarding the use of such records, some administrators have become extremely protective. There are even reported instances in which teachers are not allowed to view the students' folders but must rely instead upon summaries prepared by administrators, school counselors, or others; and some school policies stipulate that teachers can examine records only in the administrator's office.

In order to reduce this dilemma, administrators and teachers must develop trust and collaborative agreement concerning records. It should be well understood by teachers and school staff members that administrators must adhere to protecting the records and interest of students as mandated by law. On the other hand, teachers and related school staff members must have access to records in order to plan functional and realistic instructional programs and services for children with disabilities. In using accessible information, administrators should make teachers and related school staff members aware of the importance of storage, transfer, and confidentiality of students' records.

STORAGE AND TRANSFER OF STUDENTS' RECORDS

Federal and state regulations mandate that students' records be safely stored and that parental permission be sought when records are transferred. There are numerous ways of storing records, such as in folders, file cabinets, and computerized data storage. Regardless of the method of storage, administrators should have a plan for safeguarding them. This plan should reflect local, state, and federal guidelines, and developing the plan may well include evaluating and modifying the use of files by school staff members. Additionally, procedures should be modified based upon new policies, litigation, and legislation in the local, state, or federal levels.

In the Federal Register (1977) concerning transferring students' records, it was stated that

> Federal regulations specify the requirements relating to school records. First, the school must inform the parents when personally identifiable information is no longer needed to provide educational services to the child. Second, such information must be destroyed at the request of the parents. However, a record of the student's name, address, phone number, grade, attendance record, classes attended, grade level completed, and year completed may be maintained without these limitations.

Parental permission is needed to destroy any school record or testing information associated with the education of a child. Parents may request the destruction of records for a variety of reasons, such as safeguard measures, confidentiality, and improper use of records. These reasons are not inclusive. Administrators should caution parents concerning the long-term effect of requesting that records be destroyed and employ specific criteria for destroying records based upon local, state, and federal policies. Equally important is adding assessment data to the child's folder without parental permission. In order to validate new or additional information placed in children's folders, several steps should be employed.

One of the first strategies advocated by Shea and Bauer (1991) is that teachers should contact the family as soon as possible using some of the listed techniques outlined in this chapter. The benefits of this contact can be immeasurable in that parents can (1) inform the teacher about changes in the developmental sequence and test results, including the informal tests of the child, which may have an impact upon school performance; (2) assist the teacher in understanding the students' performance outside of the school that may have an impact upon performing in school; (3) shed light on cultural differences that may be impeding the instructional program; and (4) assist in reinforcing skills learned at school and monitoring homework. Data should be recorded and forwarded to parents for their agreement or disagreement. Any disagreements can be addressed at conference time (James 1996; Voor 1997).

CONFIDENTIALITY

Public Law 94-142 and the Buckley Amendment Section 513 of P.L. 93-380 mandate that information collected related to children with disabilities must be treated in a professional and confidential manner and may not be distributed without parental permission (Federal Register, 1977). Access to records by school personnel must conform to the confidentiality safeguards:

- An administrator should be appointed to monitor the use of students' records and must develop safeguard procedures for protecting them.
- Training should be provided for all school personnel regarding the use of confidentiality in using students' records.
- A list indicating all professionals in the school district who have access to confidential information must be developed and maintained.

- Records including test data must be made available for auditing and inspection as required by school policies and parental permission.
- Information electronically stored on children can easily be retrieved by individuals other than school or community personnel. This may create some problems for administrators charged with protecting confidential information. Consequently, administrators must make ethically and logically responsible decisions about informal testing data collection and storage to assure as much as possible the confidentiality of information entrusted in their care.

When the school or agency no longer needs the information, administrators must inform the parents that they have the option to request the destruction of the information. A permanent record, without regard to time constraints, involving demographic and academic information may be maintained (Taylor 2000).

REPORTING PROGRESS TO PARENTS

Parents have the right of securing information relevant to the testing, including informal testing, results of their children in school. The teacher's major responsibility is to inform parents how well their children have performed within a reporting period which has been administratively approved. Reporting periods should describe children's progress accurately and objectively. Teachers need to describe in narrative terms and provide samples of classwork so that parents can make their own assessment of their children's work (Potter 1998; Green 1998).

Teachers, as indicated, have several avenues for reporting children's testing data to parents. Before forwarding a performance report home or conducting a conference, educators should prepare an outline and include information that will reflect significant aspects of the child's behavior. Communication should be clear and concise. Language usage must be on a level the parent can understand; if the language is not native English, attempts should be made to report to the parent in his or her native language. If this is not feasible, an interpreter should be available, so that parents may effectively participate and interact with the educator. Performance reports for children with disabilities are usually long narrative descriptions of behavior, consisting of many pages.

To summarize the total report takes too much time. The educator should select the assessment he or she wishes to discuss or forward the information home to the parents for their review.

Frequently in conferences, educators and teachers have special concerns. These concerns may be completely independent of the information covered in the report. To avoid this type of encounter, educators should seek from parents their special concerns relative to assessment. Another approach would be to have a planning meeting and to set the agenda at that time, or the educator can seek permission to explore a performance that in his or her opinion is common to the parents (Goldring and Hausman 1997). Parents should keep in close contact with the school, regularly check their children's homework, and frequently send notes to the school inquiring about the performance of their children on tests, including informal tests. Parents displaying these traits are usually familiar with the school's program. These parents do not need a full conference or reporting period. Educators can simply review the major parts of the report and enlist comments from them. On the other hand, parents who do not frequently visit the school or keep in contact with it will need additional time and information concerning the school's program and reporting system.

Most parents like a reporting system that covers all aspects of human behavior in the academic, social, emotional, and physical domains. Additionally, they are seeking information relevant to classroom behavior, normative data on performance, progress reports on growth in all areas, and preferred learning styles. As outlined, teachers need to provide some parents with detailed information concerning their reporting system. Others who are well informed need little information. Educators have to decide upon the best structure for reporting performance information to parents. Teachers need to explain to parents informal testing procedures used to assess abilities in each of the listed domains (Taylor 2001).

ACADEMIC PERFORMANCE

The school should decide upon the frequencies of the reporting period; it may be monthly, quarterly, or every semester. Regardless of the reporting period, parents of children with disabilities, like all parents, are concerned about their children's academic performance in the basic skills as well as in other subjects. Teachers should provide objective information to parents in the academic areas through conferences and the reporting period. Parents should respond to the performance report. Collectively, parents and teachers can plan to develop strategies for improving the performance or plan to upgrade or remediate the deficit areas as noted from both formal and informal assessments. Planning may take place using a variety of approaches already articulated. It is the opinion of this author that a face-to-face conference is the better approach to take. The conference approach permits both teachers and parents to openly discuss their feelings and collectively plan to address the problems of the child.

SOCIAL/EMOTIONAL DEVELOPMENT

Social/emotional competency is an important aspect of relationships (Taylor 1998). Various forms of assessments may be employed to assess social competency, as noted in chapters 3 and 11. The experience of interacting with others is necessary for the welfare of all children, especially for children with disabilities. These children need to be acknowledged, noticed, valued, respected, and appreciated by others and to be aware that others want the same from them. Social/emotional competency is the sum total of one's ability to interact with other people, to take appropriate social initiatives, to understand people's reactions to one's self, and to respond accordingly (Taylor 1998). Children must learn to interact appropriately with others. Social/emotional skills are a continuous process. Parents need to know how their children's competency measures up and how they deal with their frustrations and approach new learning tasks. The teacher's performance report can indicate needed interpersonal skills to encourage and those to limit. Parental responses and practicing social skills at home can do much to augment the teacher's social skills program.

PHYSICAL DEVELOPMENT

Many children with disabilities have severe physical problems due to deficits in bones, nerves, muscles, and other organs. Many activities are restricted due to physical disabilities. Teachers should provide to parents detailed descriptions of physical activities the child can perform and provide as many physical activities as possible to assist in maintaining and developing whatever physical strength the child has. During reporting times, the teacher should discuss with the parents the strengths and weaknesses observed, and develop with them a unified plan for meeting the stated objectives for the child (Taylor 1999).

Once the child's academic, social/emotional, and physical traits have been appropriately assessed using both formal and informal instruments, the next step for teachers and parents is to decide what strategies are to be implemented to achieve the stated objectives in each of the three major areas. The classroom is an excellent place for the child to demonstrate skills in the three domains outlined and for the teacher to record and analyze data from assessment instruments (Taylor 1999).

CLASSROOM BEHAVIOR

Teachers need to make known to parents the methods and informal testing procedures that will be employed to evaluate the child's behavior and performance. This assessment requires professional judgment on the part of the teacher to accurately and objectively report the behavior. Detailed knowledge of development norms in the areas of intelligence, social/emotional, and physical development is needed in order for the teacher to make a valid report on the child's classroom behaviors. Teachers will frequently need expert assistance in assessing some of the above traits. Parents should have an opportunity to observe the child in the classroom. They should plan with the teacher strategies for improving or modifying the behaviors as noted from the assessment data. When communicating with parents relevant to classroom behaviors, the teacher can compare the performance of the child with another child of the same age using developmental milestones. However, some caution is in order. Children of the same age with disabilities and having the same disabling conditions may perform well above or below the normative group. The recommended approach would be to use the child as his or her own yardstick and assess his or her learning styles to progress over a certain timeframe.

During reporting and conference time, the teacher should discuss with the parent testing procedures used to evaluate the child, noting reasons why the child is performing above or below the expected age level of his or her peers and how the learning style was assessed. It is essential, during the conference, that the teacher accent the positive behaviors of the child and encourage the parent to reinforce those behaviors at home. For negative behaviors, strategies should be discussed to minimize or eradicate the behaviors. Before ending the discussion, reporting period, or conference teachers and parents should agree on the following:

- Decide what can be done at school and home to increase the child's performance in all areas of academic, social/emotional, and physical development.
- Develop timelines and select the location for the next conference and suggest a possible area for discussion.
- Discuss what community resources can be used to assist in meeting the stated objectives.
- Create a plan for selecting a group leader, not necessarily the teacher.
- Decide who will report to parents and to those who were not present at the initial conference.
- Leave the meeting with a tentative progress plan on how certain strategies will be achieved.

ASSESSING CHILDREN WITH DISABILITIES

The teachers become the central figures in grading and reporting procedures employed in their schools. They are exposed to pressures from parents, children, and the school's grading policies. The teacher becomes a catalyst in the grading and reporting controversy, perhaps attempting to explain the school's reporting pattern, and the unfeasibility of grading children with disabilities, to parents. Research is desperately needed to shed light on this matter. However, school administrators should make sure that parents understand the grading and reporting procedures employed and attempt to seek community support concerning the grading systems.

Reports concerning grading children with disabilities show that this activity varies from school district to school district, as well as from state to state. The use of reporting and grades in evaluating the progress of children with disabilities is highly questionable. Much of the controversy lies in the fact that educators in the past had no objective or scientific system to determine the achievement of children with disabilities. The lack of specificity and objectivity of outcomes to be graded, and the attitudes of teachers toward pupil interest and effort, decidedly reduce the validity and reliability of marks. The value of a marking system subsequently becomes dependent upon what and who is being marked, who is doing the marking, and who interprets the marks. Furthermore, marks and the accompanying competitiveness can cause many undesirable traits and attitudes to develop in children with disabilities, such as insecurity, fear, anxiety, cheating, and feelings of inferiority. These factors indicate that an objective and scientific way of evaluating the growth of these children should be instituted. Rather than group evaluation, individual evaluation based upon the unique interests, abilities, disabilities, and characteristics of exceptional children will aid in their total development. It is recommended that the approach outlined here will better provide administrators and teachers with a model that leads to effective evaluation of the children's achievement.

COLLABORATIVE EFFORTS

There is universal agreement that parents should be regularly informed by the school concerning their children's growth and development. The major source of conflict is how this progress is reported. Educators should endeavor to explain their grading systems to parents and to seek their support and approval before instituting any grading pattern. Teacher/parent conferences appear to be an opportune place to explain and seek parental approval for a marking system.

There are many ways that educators can report progress to parents. Some of these ways include report cards, use of descriptive words, checklists, narrative or letter reports, conferences, pupil self-appraisals, informal notes, telephone conversations, informal meetings, and home visits. It is maintained that as long as parents and school administrators agree upon a marking pattern, and parents understand that their children's achievement is evaluated in relation to their individual capacities, much of the controversy over marking will be significantly reduced. Reporting can then be viewed as a suitable method of helping parents to accept their children for who they are, and to understand what the school program is attempting to accomplish, and to learn how well their children are succeeding. Reporting should be a means for strengthening a sound relationship between home and school in the guidance of the child and it should contribute to increased learning (Taylor 2000).

PARENTS' INVOLVEMENT

While designing, conducting, interpreting, and paying for the assessment are the school system's responsibilities, parents have an important part to play before, during, and after the evaluation. The extent to which parents involve themselves, however, is a personal decision and will vary from family to family.

Before the evaluation, parents

- May initiate the evaluation process by requesting that the school system evaluate the child for the presence of a disability and the need for special education.
- Must be notified by the school, and give their consent, before any initial evaluation of the child may be conducted.
- May wish to talk with the person responsible for conducting the evaluation to find out what the evaluation will involve.
- May find it very useful to become informed about assessment issues in general and any specific issues relevant to their child (e.g., assessment of minority children, use of specific tests or assessment techniques with a specific disability).
- May need to advocate for a comprehensive evaluation—one that investigates all skill areas apparently affected by the suspected disability and that uses multiple means of collecting information (e.g., observations, interviews, alternative approaches).
- May suggest specific questions they would like to see addressed through the evaluation.
- Should inform the school of any accommodations the child will need (e.g., removing time limits from tests, conducting interviews/testing

in the child's native language, adapting the testing environment to the child's specific physical and other needs).

- Should inform the school if they themselves need an interpreter or other accommodations during any of their discussions with the school.
- May prepare their child for the evaluation process, explaining what will happen, and where necessary, reducing the child's anxiety. It may help the child to know that he or she will not be receiving a "grade" on the test he or she will be taking but that the purpose behind any testing is to gather information to help the student succeed in school.

During the evaluation process, parents

- Need to share with the school their insights into the child's background (developmental, medical, and academic), and past and present school performance.
- May wish to share with the school any prior school records, reports, tests, or evaluation information available on their child.
- May need to share information about cultural differences that can illuminate the educational team's understanding of the student.
- Need to make every effort to attend interviews the school may set up with them and provide information about their child.

After the evaluation, parents

- Need to carefully consider the results that emerge from their child's evaluation, in light of their own observation and knowledge of the child. Do the results make sense in terms of the behaviors, skills, needs, and attitudes they have observed in their child? Are there gaps, inconsistencies, or unexpected findings in the results that parents feel are important to address, if a comprehensive picture of the student's strengths and needs is to be developed?
- May share their insights and concerns about the evaluation results with the school and suggest areas where additional information may be needed. Schools may or may not act upon parents' suggestions,

and parents have certain recourses, under law, should they feel strongly about pursuing the matter.

- Participate fully in the development of their child's Individualized Education Program (IEP), using information from the evaluation (Waterman 1994).

SUMMARY

The teachers become the central figures in grading and reporting progress to parents. They are responsible for making sure that parents understand the assessment system and assessment techniques used in evaluating the growth of their children. Teachers and administrators should assure parents that information provided concerning their children will be safeguarded and stored appropriately and will not be released without their permission.

Parents have a right under state and federal mandates and laws to make sure that information relevant to testing and evaluating their children is well understood by them. There are many ways of reporting to parents. Some of the ways include report cards, use of descriptive words, checklists, narrative or letter reports, conferences, pupil self-appraisals, informal notes, telephone conversations, informational meetings, and home visits. Reporting to parents should be a means for strengthening a sound relationship between home and school in the guidance of the child and should stimulate the learning and growth of children.

REFERENCES

Federal Register. 1977. 42 (163), 42474–42518. Washington, D.C.: U.S. Government Printing Office.

Goldring, E. B., and C. Hausman. 1997. Empower parents for productive partnership. *Education Digest* 62, 25–29.

Green, R. 1998. A parent's perspective. *Exceptional Parents,* 28 (8), 30–32.

James, A. B. 1996. Helping the parents of a special needs child. *Lutheran Education* 132, 78–87.

Podemski, R. C., G. E. Marsh II, T. E. Smith, and B. J. Price. 1995. *Comprehensive administration of special education,* 2nd ed. Englewood Cliffs, N.J.: Prentice-Hall.

Potter, L. 1998. Making parent involvement meaningful. *Schools in the Middle* 6, 9–10.

Shea, T. M., and A. M. Bauer. 1991. *Parents and teachers of children with disabilities: A handbook for collaboration,* 2nd ed. Boston: Allyn and Bacon.

Taylor, G. R. 1998. *Curriculum strategies for teaching social skills to the disabled: Dealing with inappropriate behaviors.* Springfield, Ill.: Charles C. Thomas.

———.1999. *Curriculum models and strategies for educating children with disabilities in inclusive classrooms.* Springfield, Ill.: Charles C. Thomas.

———. 2000. *Parental involvement: A practical guide for collaboration and teamwork for students with disabilities.* Springfield, Ill.: Charles C. Thomas.

———. 2001. *Educational interventions and services for children with exceptionalities: Strategies and perspectives.* Springfield, Ill.: Charles C. Thomas.

Turnbull, H. R. 1993. *Free appropriate public education: The law and children with disabilities,* 4th ed. Reston, Va.: Love Publishing.

Voor, R. 1997. Connecting kids and parents to school. *Education Digest* 62, 20–21.

Waterman, B. B. 1994. *Assessing children for the presence of a disability.* Washington, D.C.: National Information Center for Children and Youths with Disabilities.

CHAPTER 9

Instructional Use of Assessment Data

Informal assessment techniques discussed in chapters 3 and 11 may be used to guide and assess the instructional process. Historically, these informal assessment techniques have gained wide acceptance during the last three decades; however, they were usually used after instruction to assess objectives. Teachers readily came to realize that not only the content of their tests could influence their teaching, but the content of these tests *should* influence their teaching (Popham 2002, p. 264).

Premised upon the above, educators began to use informal assessment techniques prior to instructional planning. In essence, prior use of these assessment techniques gave teachers a complete profile of students' strengths and weaknesses in various domains. Information was then used to plan the instructional program. Figure 9.1 indicates how a prior assessment model can influence the instructional program.

Instruction begins with identifying and recording the pupil's needs, interests, and so on, stating the activity and conditions under which the program will operate, as well as denoting the minimum standard that will be accepted toward the achievement of the objectives. Objectives are formulated based upon the characteristics of the children and should be both observable and measurable. From this point, objectives, testing, and instruction may all be sequenced or broken into tasks. Refining and recycling at any point in the program might be necessary, if expected pre-behaviors were not obtained, in light of postevaluative data. Negative results might be attributed to tasks not properly sequenced, to the need for revision in stating objectives, and to lack of materials or activities used in the instructional program. At any rate, the

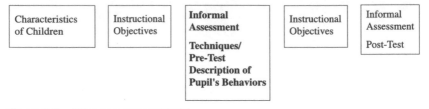

Figure 9.1.   *Prior Assessment Model*

negative alternatives should be identified before revision in the model is proposed or instruction proceeds to the next step.

Long- and short-term evaluation requires a definite statement of objectives. Evaluation concerns the extent to which goals have been reached and can only pose sensible questions when the long- and short-term goals are clearly stated (Taylor 2001). To be effective, evaluation must be a continuous process and must provide an answer to two basic questions: (1) is there evidence of pupil's growth, and (2) are the experiences received worthwhile for the children?

The proposed model is uniquely different from the traditional model. The traditional model places emphasis first on the curriculum, followed by instruction and evaluation. The major disadvantage in using the traditional model is that there is no objective way that educators can determine how well objectives have been achieved, because no attempt is made to determine prior students' skills in the subjects. On the other hand, the proposed model maintains that the success of any instructional program cannot be fully realized until some initial assessment is made before engaging students in the instructional process. It is practically impossible to determine to what degree objectives have been achieved unless some precriterion and postcriterion tests have been administered.

Pre-testing is deemed important for several reasons; it is used to

1. Determine if stated objectives are realistic and functional;
2. Guide educators in redefining objectives;
3. Provide descriptions of pupil's behavior in curriculum areas;
4. Plan for individual differences based upon the objectives and an assessed description of pupil's behaviors; and
5. Effectively plan the instructional program based upon the assessed data.

Various forms of informal assessment techniques, such as objective tests, checklists, questionnaires, rating scales, and interest inventories may be administered on a pre or post basis to determine if the objectives have been achieved and to refine the instructional program if evaluation data indicate that this is necessary (Taylor 1999, 2000).

The proposed model will assist in assuring that instructional planning will be more functional and based upon the assessed needs of children because of prior and post-assessment strategies implemented. Teachers will be better able to judge the level of skill development of children when the instruction has ended.

USE OF INFORMAL ASSESSMENT DATA

If informal assessment data are to be effectively used to gauge to what extent the stated objectives have been achieved, then they must be administered to students before and after instruction begins, to assist in

1. Evaluating the competence of a particular skill;
2. Determining the baseline behavior for a particular skill;
3. Using results to revise the unit;
4. Providing information to gauge the progress of children;
5. Appraising the effectiveness of selected skill activities;
6. Making sure that children have the necessary prerequisites for performing the skills;
7. Having the necessary physical and human resources to conduct instruction;
8. Eliciting the cooperation of parents;
9. Providing training for parents to follow-up at home;
10. Determining the reactions of children; and
11. Determining what accommodations will be needed for individuals with exceptionalities (Taylor 1998).

SPECIFIC EVALUATION TECHNIQUES

Specific evaluation techniques for evaluating the skills development of children are many. There are several informal techniques that may be applied. This section addresses informal procedures to employ. These techniques appear to be readily accessible or can be easily developed by the classroom teacher. Some recommended strategies outlined are as follows:

1. Develop a brief checklist to assess skills in a variety of situations.
2. Stimulate social, academic, and psychomotor activities requiring children to portray different roles that can be used to assess the understanding of appropriate behaviors in various settings. Group and individual appraisal of the activity may be conducted by the class.
3. Use group assignments to evaluate the ability of children to work cooperatively. Record specific incidents, both appropriate and inappropriate.
4. Model and provide illustrations of appropriate and inappropriate behaviors.
5. Structure activities and situations that call for specific kinds of behaviors and observe the performance of children. A rating scale may be used.
6. Assess the frequency of inappropriate behaviors and assist children in monitoring their own behaviors.
7. Use a variety of audiovisual aids, such as films and filmstrips depicting appropriate and inappropriate social skills, and have children critique what is taking place and give alternative responses.

Additionally, experiences and activities should be sequenced so that stated goals and objectives may be effectively achieved (Choate, Enright, Miller, Poteet, and Rakes 1995).

EVALUATING THE PUPIL'S ACHIEVEMENT

Evaluation of a pupil's progress should be an ongoing process based upon measurable and observable objectives of the instructional program. As indicated, it is of prime importance to assess prior skills before instruction is attempted. After the instructional process, pretest and post-test data should be compared and analyzed to pinpoint changes in the pupil's behavior as a result of instruction. Evaluation will also show possible needed changes in the instructional program. Lack of changes in behavior can be attributed to many factors, such as (1) program content not being relevant to children, (2) lack of materials to implement the program, (3) objectives not being stated in behavioral terms, (4) insufficient time allowed, (5) types of instruments used, (6) tasks not properly sequenced, based upon the interests, needs, and abilities of the children, and (7) poor planning and administration to effect change (Taylor 2001).

A well-planned program will have identified many ways of measuring desired changes and will lend itself to evaluation of children. The following points appear noteworthy of mention if educators are going to assess their achievements in a scientific manner:

1. The objectives must be specified in realistic and relevant terms, which will denote the behavior to be changed.
2. The characteristics, needs, interests, and abilities of the children must be identified.
3. The types of measurement to determine whether the objectives of the program were met should be clearly evident.
4. Content of the precriterion must match the postcriterion if discrepancies are to be minimized.
5. Some systematic approach should be evident for recording data.

Through the scientific approach, the end product of evaluation should reflect in behavioral changes shown by the students, that is, what the student does after the instructional program compared with what he or she initially achieved. Results from this type of evaluation will enable administrators and teachers to objectively evaluate the achievement of children, as well as reflect needed changes and modifications in the instructional program. Rubric development/assessment is also a valuable tool to evaluate and assess the progress of children.

RUBRIC ASSESSMENT

Rubrics may be used by teachers to assess the performance of children. According to Popham (2002) a rubric has three essential features. A rubric (1) identifies the evaluation criteria to be employed when judging a student's response to the task, (2) describes for each criterion how to judge qualitative differences in students' performances, and (3) indicates whether the evaluative criteria are to be applied holistically or analytically (p. 268). The evaluative criteria in a rubric may be used to identify factors that can be employed to show differences in the quality of students' responses. Rubrics may be adapted for a specific task, as indicated below. A score of four, below, reflects the highest score for completing the tasks.

Sample Rubric: Facts, Concepts, and Principles (Content) Knowledge

[4] Demonstrates a comprehensive understanding of the generalizations, concepts, and facts specific to the task or situation and provides new insights into some aspect of this information.

[3] Shows a complete and accurate understanding of the generalizations, concepts, and facts specific to completing the task.

[2] Displays an unsatisfactory understanding of the generalizations, concepts, and facts specific to the task or situation.

[1] Demonstrates severe misunderstanding about the generalizations, concepts, and facts specific to the task or situation.

The following example illustrates how this generic rubric for content knowledge could be adapted to a specific learner outcome for fourth-grade mathematics.

Outcome: The student will demonstrate understanding of how basic geometric shapes are employed in the planning of well-organized communities.

[4] Demonstrates a thorough understanding of how basic geometric shapes are used in the planning of well-organized communities and provides new insights into some aspect of their use.

[3] Displays a complete and accurate understanding of how basic geometric shapes are used in the planning of well-organized communities.

[2] Displays an incomplete understanding of how basic geometric shapes are used in the planning of well-organized communities and has some notable misconceptions about their use.

[1] Demonstrates severe misconceptions about how basic geometric shapes are used in the planning of well-organized communities.

Sample Rubric: Procedures (Content Skills)

[4] Demonstrates mastery over the strategy or skill specific to the task or situation. Can perform the strategy or skill without error and with little or no conscious effort.

[3] Carries out the strategy or skill specific to the task or situation without major error.

[2] Makes a number of mistakes when performing the strategy or skill specific to the task or situation but can complete a rough approximation of it.

[1] Makes many critical errors when performing the strategy or skill specific to the task or situation.

Notice that each scoring rubric employs a four-point scale, with 4 representing the highest level of performance, and 1 representing the lowest performance level. Educators from each district, school building, or classroom must decide what performance level will be considered acceptable. In the above sample rubrics, for example, a performance receiving a 3 would likely be the minimum acceptable level. While a 4 represents superior performance, a 1 or 2 fails to demonstrate sufficient mastery of the facts, concepts, principles, or content skills related to the specific task.

RUBRICS FOR COMPLEX THINKING PROCESSES

Determining the degree to which students utilize thinking processes represents another component of authentic task assessment. Scoring rubrics for selected complex thinking processes provide descriptive criteria for judging the level of proficiency that students demonstrate in incorporating those thinking processes into completion of the assigned task. Reliable assessment of complex thinking processes depends upon designing a scoring rubric specific for the particular thinking process being assessed within the context of the authentic task. The student may be evaluated on the following criteria.

Sample Rubric: Assessing Complex Thinking Processes.
Question: Did the student select appropriate items/elements to be compared?

[4] The student selected items that are well suited for addressing the objective outlined in the task description and that show original or creative thinking.

[3] The student selected items that provide a means for successfully addressing the objective outlined in the task description.

[2] The student selected items that satisfy the basic requirements of the task description but create some difficulties for executing the task.

[1] The student selected items that are inappropriate or that create insurmountable problems for the accomplishment of the task objective.

Assessors would have to design a similar scoring rubric for each of the other evaluation criteria associated with the comparing process. They would also have to decide which proficiency level would represent the minimal acceptable standard.

RUBRICS FOR LEARNER EXIT OUTCOMES

Learner exit outcomes describe in broad terms the knowledge, skills, and attitudes students must demonstrate by the time they graduate. Several proficiencies or performance indicators identified for each exit outcome provide a basis for determining to what degree students have achieved the broader exit outcomes.

Since learner exit outcomes represent cumulative achievement over longer periods of time, they need only be assessed annually and prior to graduation. However, scoring rubrics similar to those described for learner outcomes and complex thinking processes still offer an excellent vehicle for assessing learner exit outcome proficiencies.

A specific scoring rubric using descriptive criteria should be designed for each exit outcome proficiency to enable a reliable assessment of the proficiency. The following illustrates an example of a scoring rubric for the proficiency and sets priorities and achievable goals associated with the learner exit outcome of self-directed learning (Wiggins 1993a, 1993b; Stiggins 1994; Marzano, Pickering, and McTighe 1993).

Exit Outcomes—Evaluation Criteria

[4] Consistently develops clear, challenging expectations and goals; has a clear sense of his or her own physical, mental, and emotional abilities, and strives to work close to the edge of competence.

[3] Perceives the value of goals and their accomplishment.

[2] Shows maturity of judgment in the establishment of priorities.

[1] Establishes the criteria for success before beginning work.

Constructing and scoring rubrics can be a time-consuming process. Teachers may use several approaches and should be knowledgeable about several evaluative criteria to use to describe and score rubrics. Various levels are needed to describe performance levels. The issues of rubric construction and use are fully summarized in chapter 5.

SUMMARY

The importance and values of implementing an informal assessment prior to planning an instructional program are summarized in this chapter. Assessment should guide the instructional program, not the instructional program dictating the type of assessment to be used. The importance of objectives in the instructional program was also highlighted, with a model demonstrating that classroom assessment should be created before instructional planning. Instructional planning should be based upon the data yielded from classroom or informal assessment.

REFERENCES

Choate, J., B. Enright, L. Miller, J. Poteet, and R. Rakes. 1995. *Curriculum assessment and programming,* 3rd ed. Boston: Allyn and Bacon.

Marzano, R. J., D. J. Pickering, and J. McTighe. 1993. *Assessing student outcomes: Performance assessment using the dimensions of learning model.* Alexandria, Va.: Association for Supervision and Curriculum Development.

Popham, W. J. 2002. *Classroom assessment: What do teachers need to know?* Boston: Allyn and Bacon.

Stiggins, R. J. 1994. *Student-centered classroom assessment.* New York: Merrill.

Taylor, G. R. 1998. *Curriculum strategies for teaching social skills to the disabled.* Springfield, Ill.: Charles C. Thomas.

———. 1999. *Curriculum models and strategies for educating individuals with disabilities in inclusive classrooms.* Springfield, Ill.: Charles C. Thomas.

———. 2001. *Educational interventions and services for children with exceptionalities: Strategies and perspectives.* Springfield, Ill.: Charles C. Thomas.

Wiggins, G. 1993a. Assessment, authenticity, content, and validity. *Phi Delta Kappan*, 200–214.

———. 1993b. *Assessing student performance: Exploring the purpose and limits of testing.* San Francisco: Jossey-Bass.

CHAPTER 10

Grading Using Informal Assessment

Several research studies have examined the grading practices of schools as related to assessing children (Olson 1995, Tyack and Tobin 1994; Guskey 1996; Cross and Frary 1999). Generally these studies have shown that the reform movement and the public outcry for improved grading practices had a significant impact on examining our present grading patterns and instituting reforms. When standard grading practices are employed, some individual teachers may include at their own discretion different nonachievement factors in assigning grades.

A study of mainstreamed children with disabilities in the sixth and eighth grades concerning letter grades revealed that these children felt helpless in attempts to earn high grades but blamed themselves for the low grades (Selby and Murphy 1992). Normal standards were applied in grading these students (Putnam 1992). Research found that teacher-made tests in science, social studies, math, and English did not address higher thinking or critical thinking skills. The questions were frequently written in the multiple-choice format and were asked at the knowledge level. Questions written at this level do little to stimulate critical thinking skills for children, especially those with disabilities. The major question that educators may face concerning grading students is whether or not standard grading practices are effective in assessing the performances of children, including those with disabilities.

GRADING AND INSTRUCTION

Grades indicate to teachers students' strengths and weaknesses in content subjects. They are also frequently used to group children for instruction and by teachers as a planning instrument (Marzano 2000). It is assumed that the same skills unique to a specific content area are taught by different teachers using the same textbooks and resources. Recent research findings have disputed the above. Findings indicate that individual teachers may not adequately cover the stated content and that at the conclusion of a grade no one is exactly sure what students have been exposed to (Doyle 1992; Stodolsky 1989).

In support of the above findings, Stevenson and Stigler (1992) observe the following:

> Daunted by the length of most textbooks and knowing that the children's future teachers will be likely to return to the material, American teachers often omit some topics. Different topics are omitted by different teachers thereby making it impossible for the children's later teacher to know what has been covered at earlier grades—they cannot be sure what their students know and do not know. (p. 140)

Local and state educational agencies rapidly recognized the problems and have instituted standards in all of the content areas that all teachers are mandated to follow and use in their grading practices. Informal assessment instruments must reflect indicators in the standards.

PURPOSE OF GRADES

In addition to instructional planning, grades are used for (1) administrative purposes, (2) to give students feedback about their progress and achievement, (3) to provide guidance to students about future coursework, and (4) to motivate students (Wrinkle 1947; Airasian 1994; Austin and McCann 1992). All types of informal assessment techniques are used to provide grades as discussed in chapters 3 and 11.

Administrative

Grades have been administratively used to determine student matriculation and retention, placement of students, transferring students, student entrance into college, student rank in class, promotion, and credits for graduation. A survey conducted by the College Board (1998) revealed that 81 percent of schools used grades for administrative purposes.

Feedback About Student Achievement

One of the primary purposes of grades is to provide feedback relevant to student achievement. As early as 1976, survey data indicated that both educators and noneducators believed that providing information about student achievement is a prime purpose of grading (Simon and Bellanca 1976). Surveys conducted in 1989 and 1992 showed similar results (Stiggins, Frisbie, and Griswold 1989; Austin and McCann 1992).

Guidance

Guidance is also an important purpose for grades. Grades are used by counselors and school personnel to guide students in the areas of course selection, occupations to consider, and college admission. A significant number of teachers and counselors consider guidance as an important purpose for grades.

Motivation

Grades have been used to motivate students to higher levels of achievement. It is assumed that receiving a higher grade will motivate students to continue their efforts. Austin and McCann (1992) report that approximately 32 percent of educators emphasized motivation as a purpose for grades.

CLASSROOM ASSESSMENT

In chapters 3 and 11 various informal techniques and devices are outlined with specific instructions for constructing them. Designing a rubric is not difficult because rubrics tend to follow general patterns. The logic underlying the generic rubric according to Marzano (2000) is fairly straightforward. At level 4, students understand the important information accurately and in detail. At level 3, they understand the important information accurately but not in detail. At level 2, students have an incomplete understanding and/or have some misconceptions about important information.; however, they still know enough to have a basic understanding of the topic. At level 1, students have so many misconceptions or their knowledge is so incomplete that they cannot be said to possess an understanding of the topic. Finally, a score of 0 indicates that the student provided little or no information with which to make a judgment. See chapters 3 and 11 for additional details on constructing and evaluating rubrics.

GRADING CHILDREN WITH DISABILITIES

Reporting the progress of children with disabilities to parents may require some modification in the regular grading procedures. Administrators can make modifications based upon the unique disability and interest of the child if needed. Many children with disabilities will not need any modifications in the grading procedures used. Any modifications made should resemble the regular grading system as much as possible. Strickland and Turnbull (1993) conclude that maintaining similar grading procedures for all students can serve to protect the student's right to confidentiality. State guidelines contain little information on grading. Most states give local school districts the authority to decide how children with disabilities will be graded. However, some states are reviewing their grading policies.

It is incumbent upon administrators to develop effective reporting procedures for informing parents of the progress of their children with disabilities. A first step will be for administrators to examine state and local regulations concerning grading practices. Reporting to parents can also improve communication between the home and school. There are several reporting techniques that administrators and teachers can employ to inform parents. These techniques are chosen based upon the disabilities, needs, and interests of exceptional children, and they are by no means inclusive. Reporting techniques include the following:

1. Anecdotal Records. Anecdotal records may be used to show progress of students. A permanent type of folder should be used such as a spiral notebook to keep information. All relevant infor-

mation concerning the student can be listed and categorized. Information listed in anecdotal records may provide information needed to justify a change in the student's academic program. Teachers should attempt to control their own subjectivity in their interpretation of behaviors.

2. Work Samples. Work samples are excellent to use in comparing a student's performance between time periods on any area or areas in his or her academic program. Students can plot their own progress by using work samples. Parents can also have an objective method to gauge their children's progress in school.

3. Checklist. The teacher records critical behaviors he or she has observed in the educational setting. Information is forwarded home to the parents. The parents' signature denotes that they have read the information included in the checklist. Collective strategies can be developed by the teacher and the parents to reduce or eliminate the undesirable behavior or in some instances to promote a desirable behavior.

4. Newsletters. A newsletter is an excellent communication device for apprising parents about school issues and special events to be conducted at the school. The newsletter is an excellent device for seeking cooperation from parents in conducting certain school functions.

5. Daily or Weekly Report Cards. These report cards inform parents about the academic progress of their children. Parents have an opportunity to respond to the report cards and to indicate ways in which they can assist the child or to make other relevant comments.

6. Telephone Calls. Most telephone calls to parents are negative, but they can be a useful tool for positive communication as well.

7. An Award System. This system awards children for their accomplishments. The nature of the disability and the interests and needs of the children are considered. No group standards are employed. The child becomes his or her own yardstick and is awarded based upon achieving his or her individualized objectives.

8. Use of Cameras and Videotapes. The behaviors of students are recorded with the permission of parents. The recordings and pictures may be used by the teacher and parents to reinforce positive behaviors or to remediate negative behaviors.

9. Use of Computer Technology. This technology affords rapid reporting to parents, providing the parents have the necessary computer hardware and software and are versed in their uses.
10. Home Visits. Conditions in some communities do not make home visits an attractive option to many teachers. Some teachers, in spite of poor community conditions, visit homes. It is recommended if home visits are conducted in most urban communities that homes be visited before dark and that another individual accompany the teacher.

One of the first strategies advocated by Shea and Bauer (1991) and Taylor (2000) is that teachers should contact parents as soon as possible, using some of the techniques outlined above. The benefits of this contact can be immeasurable in that parents can (1) inform the teacher about changes in the developmental sequence of the child, (2) clarify questions relative to the informal assessment tools used, (3) ask for explanation on how grading was conducted, and (4) provide approval of the grade techniques used.

SUMMARY

Teachers become the central figures in grading and reporting procedures employed in the schools. They are exposed to pressures from parents, children, administrators, and the community at large concerning their grading policies. To reduce these pressures, the school should make sure that parents are involved in, and understand, the grading and reporting system used.

Reports for children with disabilities deviate from school district to school district, as well as from state to state. The present standard used in evaluating the progress of children with disabilities is highly questionable. The use of informal techniques, where children's abilities are judged on intra-individual differences, will do much to improve the controversy over grading of children with disabilities. Through using informal assessment techniques to evaluate and assign grades, teachers can have more control and objectivity in assigning grades.

REFERENCES

Airasian, P. W. 1994. *Classroom assessment,* 2nd ed. New York: McGraw-Hill.

Austin, S., and R. McCann. 1992. *Here's another arbitary grade for your collection: A statewide study of grading policies.* Paper presented at the Annual Meeting of the American Educational Resource Association. San Francisco: ERIC Document Reproduction Service No. 343944.

College Board. 1998. *High school grading policies.* Research notes: RN-02. Princeton, N.J: College Board.

Cross, L. H., and R. B. Frary. 1999. Hodge podge grading: Endorsed by students and teachers alike. *Applied Measurement in Education* 12 (1), 53–72.

Doyle, W. 1992. Curriculum and pedagogy. In P. W. Jackson, ed., *Handbook of Research in Currriculum* (pp. 465–85). New York: Macmillan.

Guskey, T. R. 1996. Reporting on student learning: Lessons from the past— prescriptions for the future. In T. R. Guskey, ed., *Communicating Student Learning* (1996 ASCD Yearbook, pp. 13–24). Alexandria, Va.: Association for Supervision and Curriculum Development.

Marzano, R. J. 2000. *Transforming classroom gradings.* Alexandria, Va.: Association for Supervision and Curriculum Development.

Olson, L. 1995. Cards on the table. *Education Week,* 23–28.

Putnam, M. L. 1992. Characteristics of questions on test administered by mainstream secondary classroom teachers. *Learning Disabilities Research and Practice* 7 (3), 29–36.

Selby, D., and S. Murphy. 1992. Graded or degraded: Perceptions of letter-grading for mainstreamed learning-disabled students. *British Columbia Journal of Special Education* 16 (1), 92–104.

Shea, T. M., and A. M. Bauer. 1991. *Parents and teachers of children with exceptionalities: A handbook for collaboration,* 2nd ed. Boston: Allyn and Bacon.

Simon, S. B., and J. A. Bellanca, eds. 1976. *Regarding the grading myths: Primer of alternatives to grades and marks.* Alexandria, Va.: Association for Supervision and Curriculum Development.

Stevenson, H. W., and J. W. Stigler. 1992. *The learning gap: Why our schools are failing and what we can learn from Japanese and Chinese education.* New York: Touchstone.

Stiggins, R. J., D. A. Frisbie, and P. A. Griswold. 1989. Inside high school grading practices: Building a research agenda. *Educational Measurements Issues and Practices* 8 (2), 5–14.

Stodolsky, S. S. 1989. Is teaching really by the books? In P. W. Jackson and S. Haroutunian-Gordon, eds., *Eighty-ninth yearbook of the national society for the study of education,* part I (pp. 159–84). Chicago: University of Chicago Press.

Strickland, B. B., and A. D. Turnbull. 1993. *Developing and implementing individualized education programs.* Englewood Cliffs, N.J.: Prentice-Hall.

Taylor, G. R. 2000. *Parental involvement: A practical guide for students with disabilities.* Springfield, Ill.: Charles C. Thomas.

Tyack, T., and W. Tobin. 1994. The "grammar" of schooling: Why has it been so hard to change? *American Educational Research Journal* 31 (3), 453–79.

Wrinkle, W. L. 1947. *Improving marking and reporting practices in elementary and secondary schools.* New York: Holt, Rinehart, and Winston.

CHAPTER 11

Assessing Individuals with Disabilities

Most of the informal tests discussed in this text can be adapted or modified for individuals with disabilities. These disabilities constitute a wide range of behaviors, and teachers may need assistance in assessing some of the areas. Assessment in an educational setting serves five primary purposes:

1. Screening and identification to screen children and identify those who may be experiencing delays or learning problems;
2. Eligibility and diagnosis to determine whether a child has a disability and is eligible for special education services, and to diagnose the specific nature of the student's problems or disability;
3. Individualized Education Program (IEP) development and placement to provide detailed information so that an IEP may be developed and appropriate decisions may be made about the child's special needs; and
4. Evaluation to evaluate student progress (refer to chapter 7) (Berdine and Meyer 1987, p. 5).

Assessment is a complex process and involves several important steps in assessing children with exceptionalities and includes (1) screening, (2) referral, (3) determining eligibility, (4) program planning, (5) program monitoring, and (6) program evaluation. School districts may interpret or use their own procedures to expand or modify the steps. To assist school districts in clarifying the steps, Cohen and Spenciner (1998) have comprehensively outlined procedures to employ, and graphic and narrative descriptions are given for each step. Specific attention will be given to these topics later in the text.

While these children are different from each other in very many ways, they may also share something in common. Each may be a student who has a disability that will require special education services in the school setting. Before decisions may be made about what those special education services will be, each child will require an evaluation conducted by specially trained educational personnel, which may include a school psychologist, a speech/language pathologist, special education and regular education teachers, social workers, and, when appropriate, medical personnel. This is true for any child suspected of having a difficulty (Waterman 1994).

IDENTIFYING STUDENTS FOR ASSESSMENT

Teachers are usually the first education personnel to identify children with disabilities for assessment. They employ a variety of informal techniques, such as observations; interviews; and evaluation of performance on tests, students' work, and grades. Chapters 2, 3, and 5 overview these informal techniques. Frequently some amendments and adaptations will need to be made in the tests to accommodate the diverse needs of the children. In constructing and using informal assessment techniques to assess children with disabilities, teachers should make sure that

1. The children understand the mode of communication.
2. The children are familiar with the format of the text.
3. The test is written in the child's primary language.
4. Approved and appropriate accommodations are present.
5. Parental permission is given for testing.
6. The informal instrument is appropriate for the child.
7. Test items are similar to classroom tasks.
8. Test items are related to information covered in class.

Assessing, identifying, and placing children in the least restrictive environment requires the use of nondisciplinary and multidisciplinary assessment in developing the IEP (Taylor 1998; Thurlow, Elliott, and

Ysseldyke 1998). Once educational need is established through formal and informal testing, the student is referred to a multidisciplinary team. Based upon the type of data assessed by the team, the student's ability is defined and classified.

MULTIDISCIPLINARY TEAM MEMBERSHIP

The team must include a "teacher or other specialist with knowledge in the areas of suspected disability" (34 CFR 300.533). In practice, diagnosticians and parents are usually members of multidisciplinary teams (MDTs). Informal information supplied by the teacher is essential for the team to operate.

RESPONSIBILITIES OF THE MULTIDISCIPLINARY TEAM

Salvia and Ysseldyke (1998) write that the team is responsible for gathering information and making a recommendation about a student's exceptionality. The teacher's recommendations are usually expressed through the use of informal data submitted. In theory, the decision-making process is straightforward. The MDT assesses the student's performance to see whether it meets the criteria for a specific exceptionality. It must collect information required by the definition of exceptionality. Federal regulations (34 CFR 300.533) also require the team to do the following:

1. Draw on information from a variety of sources, including aptitude and achievement tests, teacher's recommendations, physical conditions, social or cultural background, and adaptive behavior.
2. Ensure that information obtained from all of these sources is documented and carefully considered.

Team members should be competent in the areas they assess. They should be certified or licensed in their respective disciplines. The focus of assessment is to determine the nature and type of exceptionality, type of placement, how well the student is meeting the stated goals and objectives, and related services needed.

DEVELOPING INFORMAL ASSESSMENT DEVICES

It has been indicated throughout this text that teachers must be aware of several informal devices as well as know how to modify and adapt them for use with children with disabilities. Popham (2002) inferred that the more teachers understand the development and construction of tests, the more effectively they can use that understanding to clarify what's to be sought instructionally (p. 14). Popham further stated that the classroom assessment instruments should always be prepared prior to any instructional planning in order for the teacher to better understand what is being sought of students, and therefore, what to incorporate in instructional activities for students.

Teachers of children with disabilities, as well as teachers of children in general, will need to know how to develop and analyze a variety of informal techniques, as highlighted in chapters 3, 7, and 9. Teachers need to judge to what degree children have mastered the objectives and to determine the student's attitudes toward the subject. Additionally, teachers need to be aware of the connection between testing and teaching when developing informal or teacher-made tests. It is of prime importance when developing informal tests that teachers consider the disabilities of the children. For example, an essay-type test would not be suited for most children with cerebral palsy. The teacher will need to determine the learning styles of children so that test items and response modes will be matched to suit children's needs.

Teacher-made and informal tests may be used to supplement or compare results from standardized tests. They are designed to determine how well children have met the stated objectives. They also may be employed where standardized tests are not adequate for reasons of content, difficulty, scope, or sensitive cultural materials. Teacher made-tests should be based on objectives of the course. One of the first things a teacher should consider in constructing a test is the type of test format to be employed. There are several types of testing formats as reported in chapter 3: (1) true-false, (2) multiple-choice, (3) matching, (4) completion, and (5) essay. The type of format chosen will greatly depend upon the disabling conditions of the children being tested. Several adaptations and modifications may need to be made in the testing command and response (Taylor 2001).

A variety of teacher-made informal assessment devices and techniques are at the disposal of the classroom teacher, such as observations, questionnaires, interviews, and inventories (refer to appendix A). Informal assessment provides information relevant to the student's current level of performance and assists in pinpointing goals, objectives, and needed adaptation and modification in the instructional program. Student performance is compared to specific learning tests or objectives within the curriculum. These techniques permit the direct assessment of student behaviors, which may be compared with norm-referenced test data. They may be adapted for use with children who have disabilities.

ACCOMMODATING PUPILS

In chapter 3, brief attention was given to accommodating individuals with disabilities. This section provides additional details concerning accommodations. Accommodations are designed to reduce the effect of pupil characteristics that are not related to the primary focus of the test (Airasian 2001). Examples may include the following: if a pupil has a hearing disability that may interfere with performance on an oral test, the pupil may be provided with a written test; or, a pupil who is new to the English language may be given the test in his or her own language, and if the test must be taken in English, the pupil may be given extra time to complete the test (Taylor 2001).

Most states have developed their own list of accommodations that teachers can use providing that they are listed in the Individual Education Plan (IEP) in the following categories:

1. Modifying the presentation format involves changing the format of the test to accommodate the disabilities of the children. Strategies include reading test items slowly; providing oral directions; listing directions slowly and in sequential steps; having pupils repeat directions to ensure clarity and understanding; reading test; questions to children; placing each sentence on a separate line; providing Braille, large print, sign language, native language, or bilingual language; and revising or simplifying language level.

2. Modifying the response format permits teachers to provide a variety of resources to children to respond to test items. Resources may include using dictionaries, calculators, and texts, or permitting students to use Braille, large print, and sign language. Native language and tape recorders may be permitted when listed in the IEP. Modifying the response format may include providing verbal prompts, providing a scribe, providing examples of expected test responses (this does not imply "teaching the test," but using similar test items and concepts), providing an outline for essay items, providing definitions or formulas for the pupil, allowing the use of notes, double-checking pupils' understanding of the items and desired responses, and making the test similar to what was taught to children.

3. Modifying test timing implies that educators have the flexibility to alter the time for children to complete the test. Some examples include providing extra time for children to complete the test, staying away from timed tests, testing over a period of discrete testing sections (divide the test into as many sections as needed for the children to complete it). Teachers may give extra breaks during testing and allow unlimited time for children to complete the test.

4. Modifying test setting involves changing the testing situation to a more suitable location. Educators may test children in a separate and quiet location, arrange children's seats away from noise and distractions, and test pupils individually.

When using accommodations, teachers should not attempt to draw undue attention to children when testing them. Some recommended strategies may be to conduct private conferences, make accommodations as normal as possible, be sensitive to the feelings of children with disabilities, and provide some of the same assistance given to children with disabilities as their peers. The same guidelines proposed in chapter 4 about preparing students for informal tests may be used with children with disabilities, providing accommodations, modifications, and adaptations are considered.

SUMMARY

Informal tests are sometimes necessary to accommodate the variety of conditions presented by individuals with disabilities. Accommodations may take many forms, such as changes in the length of the test, changing test items, different testing formats, the test setting, small groups, individual testing, simplification of directions, and developing vocabulary and directions in the students' native language, and they may all be necessary, to appropriately assess children with disabilities. Informal tests may be used to validate or support findings from several test types used. A checklist may be used to validate information from a rating scale.

Since more informal tests do not meet the standardization procedures employed in standardized tests, validity and reliability have not been established. Consequently, many of the procedures are recognized as subjective. Educators may employ several strategies to make informal tests more objective, such as:

1. Developing training sessions orienting teachers to the assessment task;
2. Having a consensus among raters about the meaning of assessment criteria and scoring;
3. Inter-rater reliability to reach acceptable levels of percentage agreement; and
4. Checking rater consistency across years.

Informal testing procedures, as stated, may be used to support assessment data from standardized tests. Many children with disabilities do not have the mental, physical, or social development to attend successfully to standardized procedures. Through the use of informal measures the playing field is made more even for children with disabilities. The major question facing educators who wish to use informal tests is one of validity and reliability. The four steps outlined above will do much to improve the validity and reliability of these measures.

Perrone (1991) writes that student evaluation is basic to student growth. School districts have attempted to meet this goal by depending upon a variety of standardized tests, which may not provide educators with sufficient information to conduct the academic program. Other types of assessment practices should include (1) information from cumulative records, (2) open-ended formats, which may include the use of open-ended questionnaires, self-reporting, and surveys, (3) a variety of settings employed to collect data, (4) practices based upon a theoretical framework, such as developmental milestones to assess behaviors, and (5) the use of teacher-constructed instruments to assess students in most academic, social, and physical traits (present trends strongly support this practice).

REFERENCES

Airasian, P. W. 2001. *Classroom assessment: Concepts and applications*. New York: McGraw Hill.

Berdine, W. H., and S. A. Meyer. 1987. *In special education*. Boston: Little, Brown and Company.

Cohen, L. G., and L. J. Spenciner. 1998. *Assessment of children and youth*. New York: Addison Wesley Longman.

Perrone, V. 1991. *Expanding student assessment*. Alexandria, Va.: Association for Supervision and Curriculum Development.

Popham, W. J. 2002. *Classroom assessment: What do teachers need to know?* Boston: Allyn and Bacon.

Salvia, J., and J. E.Ysseldyke. 1998. *Assessment*. Boston: Houghton-Mifflin.

Taylor, G. R. 1998. *Curriculum strategies for teaching social skills to the disabled: Dealing with inappropriate behaviors*. Springfield, Ill.: Charles C. Thomas.

———. 2001. *Educational interventions and services for children with exceptionalities: Strategies and perspectives*. Springfield, Ill.: Charles C. Thomas.

Thurlow, M. L., J. L. Elliott, and J. E. Ysseldyke. 1998. *Testing students with disabilities: Practical strategies for complying with district and state requirements*. Thousand Oaks, Calif.: Corwin Press.

Waterman, B. B. 1994. *Assessing children for the presence of a disability*. Washington, D.C.: National Information Center for Children and Youth with Disabilities.

CHAPTER 12

Concluding Remarks

Cohen and Spenciner (1998) articulate that *assessment* is a global term for observing, gathering, recording, and interpreting information to answer questions and make legal instructional decisions about students. In essence, assessment is used to make valid decisions about students in areas of learning and human functioning. Assessment is a multifaceted process, which involves more than the use of standardized tests. Informal tests can yield valuable information used in assessment. The process includes assessing individuals in a variety of mental, physical, and social tasks (Taylor 2000).

DEFINING ASSESSMENT

There is some time confusion regarding the terms *assessment* and *testing*. While they are related, they are not synonymous. Testing is the administration of specifically designed measures of behavior and is part of the assessment process. Assessment, also known as evaluation, can be seen as a problem-solving process (Swanson and Watson 1989) that involves many ways of collecting information about the student. Roth-Smith (1991) suggests that this information-gathering process should involve the following formal and informal techniques:

- Observing the student's interactions with parents, teachers, and peers;
- Interviewing the student and significant others in his or her life;
- Examining school records and past evaluation reports;
- Evaluating developmental and medical histories;

- Using information from checklists completed by parents, teachers, or the student;
- Evaluating curriculum requirements and options;
- Evaluating the student's type and rate of learning during trial teaching periods;
- Using task analysis to identify which task components already have been mastered and in what order unmastered skills need to be taught; and
- Collecting ratings on teacher attitudes toward students with disabilities, peer acceptance, and classroom climate (Roth-Smith 1991, p. 307).

Clearly, gathering information about the student using such a variety of techniques and information sources can be expected to shed considerable light upon the student's strengths and needs, the nature of his or her disability, and how it affects educational performance, and what type of instructional goals and objectives should be established for the student.

CHOOSING APPROPRIATE INFORMAL ASSESSMENT

In chapters 3 and 11 a variety of informal assessment instruments were summarized. From this list teachers may choose or develop their own instruments. However, a word of caution is in order. The type of informal instrument chosen should be appropriate for the student. Teachers may use interviews and observation to assist them in choosing and developing appropriate informal assessment instruments. The following strategies and considerations are recommended to assist teachers:

1. Consider the skill areas to be assessed and identify the type of informal testing format to use.
2. Is the content area being assessed appropriate for the student?
3. What is the specific purpose of the informal assessment?
4. What accommodations, if any, are needed?
5. Are there available human and physical resources to provide accommodations?
6. How similar are the informal test contents to actual classroom tasks?

7. What is the relationship of the tests to objectives and mandated standards?

GATHERING ASSESSMENT INFORMATION

The child must be assessed "in all areas related to the suspected disability, including, if appropriate, health, vision, hearing, social and emotional status, general intelligence, academic performance, communicative status, and motor abilities." (Taylor, 2002, p. 191)

Because of the convenient and plentiful nature of standardized tests, it is perhaps tempting to administer a battery (group) of tests to a student and make an eligibility or placement determination based upon the results. However, tests alone will not give a comprehensive picture of how a child performs or what he or she knows or does not know. Evaluators need to use a variety of tools and approaches to assess a child, including observing the child in different settings to see how he or she functions in those environments, interviewing individuals who know the child to gain their insights, and testing the child to evaluate his or her competence in whatever skill areas appear affected by the suspected disability, as well as in possible areas of strength.

There are, recently, a number of other approaches being used to collect information about students as well; these include curriculum-based assessment, ecological assessment, task analysis, dynamic assessment, and assessment of learning style. These approaches yield rich information about students, are especially important when assessing students from culturally or linguistically diverse backgrounds, and, therefore, are critical methods in the overall approach to assessment. Students possessing medical or mental health problems may also have assessment information from sources outside of the school. Such information would need to be considered along with assessment information from the school's evaluation team in making appropriate diagnoses, placement decisions, and instructional plans.

Only through collecting data using a variety of informal approaches and from a variety of sources (parents, teachers, specialists, peers, the student) can an adequate picture be obtained of the child's strengths and weaknesses. Synthesized, this information can be used to determine the specific nature of the child's special needs and whether the child needs special services, and if so, to design an appropriate program.

REVIEWING SCHOOL RECORDS

School records can be a rich source of information about a student and his or her background. The number of times the student has changed schools may be of interest; frequent school changes can be disruptive emotionally as well as academically and may be a factor in the problems that have resulted in the student's being referred for assessment. Attendance is another area to note; are there patterns in absences (e.g., during a specific part of the year, as is the case with some students who have respiratory problems or allergies), or is there a noticeable pattern of declining attendance, which may be linked to a decline in motivation, an undiagnosed health problem, or a change within the family?

The student's past history of grades is usually of interest to the assessment team as well. Is the student's current performance in a particular subject typical of the student, or is the problem being observed something new (Waterman 1994)?

Test scores from assessment instruments are also important to review, including data from informal assessments. These assessment data may indicate strengths and weaknesses in several curriculum domains. Based upon those results a realistic and functional instructional plan can be developed (Hoy and Gregg 1994, p. 37; Taylor 2001).

APPROACHES TO ASSESSMENT

Assessment is a complex process that needs to be conducted by a multidisciplinary team of trained professionals and involves both formal and informal methods of collecting information about the student. While the team may choose to administer a series of tests to the student, by law, assessment must involve much more than standardized tests. Interviews of all key participants in the student's education and observations of student behaviors in the classroom or in other sites should be included as well. To develop a comprehensive picture of the student and to develop practical intervention strategies to address that student's special needs, the team must ask questions and use informal assessment techniques that will help them determine the factors that are facilitating and interfering with the child's learning. Ecological assessment, dynamic assessment, curriculum-based assessment, learning styles inventories, and other less traditional approaches may be particularly helpful in answering such questions (Taylor 2001).

It is also important that assessment be an ongoing process. The process begins even before the student is referred for informal evaluation; his or her teachers or parents may have noticed that some aspect of the student's performance or behavior is below expectations and requested an official assessment.

Individuals with disabilities are constantly being assessed to determine services and placement. Information from an assessment device seldom provides the special educator with specific remediation strategies for instructing the children, or a complete assessment of the student's strengths and weaknesses in specific areas. There is an urgent need to train teachers to develop teacher-made and informal tests to augment results from standardized tests. Additionally, special educators should be competent in the use of techniques for providing accommodations for children with disabilities (Taylor 2002).

The role of parental and community involvement in assessment must be given careful consideration. Parents can provide valuable information by identifying strengths and weaknesses of their children. Federal and state laws mandate that parental permission be given before any assessment is conducted or any assessment data is released to individuals or agencies (Taylor 2000).

The focus of assessment is to provide information from which the team can determine the nature and type of disability, type of placement, and related services needed. To achieve these outcomes specialists from several disciplines may be needed, depending upon the disabling conditions of the child being assessed.

Assessment involves evaluating students' competencies in academics, personality traits, and physical abilities to determine how well they have achieved a standard. Assessment involves gathering information to make valid decisions concerning the behavior of individuals. When assessing children with disabilities many tests and assessment devices will have to be modified to accommodate the severe needs of these children. Several specialists may be needed to assist in the process.

REFERENCES

Cohen, L. G., and L. J. Spenciner. 1998. *Assessment of children and youth.* New York: Addison Wesley Longman.

Hoy, C., and N. Gregg. 1994. *Assessment: The special educator's role.* Pacific Grove, Calif.: Brooks/Cole.

Roth-Smith, C. 1991. *Learning disabilities: The interaction of learner, task, and setting.* Boston: Allyn and Bacon.

Swanson, H. C., and B. L. Watson. 1989. *Educational and logical assessment of exceptional children,* 2nd ed. Columbus, Ohio: Merrill.

Taylor, G. R. 2000. *Parental involvement.* Springfield, Ill.: Charles C. Thomas.

———. 2001. *Educational interventions and services for children with exceptionalities: Strategies and perceptions.* Springfield, Ill.: Charles C. Thomas.

———. 2002. *Assessing children with disabilities.* New York: Edwin Mellen Press.

Waterman, B. B. 1994. *Assessing children in the presence of a disability.* Washington, D.C.: National Information Center for Children and Youth with Disabilities.

Observation Checklist

Teacher_____   Observer_____
Lesson_____   Date_____ Time_____

KEY: A = Always   F = Frequently   N = Never

BEHAVIORS	A	F	N
Student deals positively with accusations.			
Student accepts apologies from others.			
Student respects the feelings of others.			
Student knows how to avoid fights and conflicts and displays good humor.			
Student deals effectively with teasing.			
Student moves about room independently to perform routine tasks.			
Student stays away from troublesome situations and accepts cultural values of other pupils.			
Student verbally shows appreciation when assisted.			
Student gives praise or compliments to other students.			
Student accepts compliments from others.			
Student apologizes for inappropriate behavior.			
Student expresses anger in a positive way.			
Student attempts to understand another's anger without getting angry.			
Student shows affection and appreciation toward others.			
Student asks permission to borrow or use other's belongings.			
Students does not lose control when left out of group activities.			
Student practices self-control.			
Student disagrees in an acceptable manner.			
Student accepts losing without becoming upset.			

A Sample Rubric Assessment Sheet

Criteria for Evaluation	Evaluation	Weight	Score
Understanding and use of topic-specific information:		1/3/5	
Did the student understand the content area facts, concepts, and principles important to the task?	1 2 3 4	_____	_____
Did the student effectively use the content skills and processes important to the task?	1 2 3 4	_____	_____
Use of the process of classification:			
Did the student use all important components of the process necessary to complete the task?	1 2 3 4	_____	_____
Were the elements identified for classification important to the topic?	1 2 3 4	_____	_____
Were the categories the student selected to organize the elements useful and important?	1 2 3 4	_____	_____
Were the defining characteristics of the categories important and useful?	1 2 3 4	_____	_____
Did the student accurately access the extent to which each element possesses each defining characteristic?	1 2 3 4	_____	_____

Assessor _____   OVERALL SCORE= _____

Learning Outcomes and Informal
Methods of Evaluation

Types of Behavior	Evaluation Methods
Application	Objective Tests, Rating Scales, Checklists
Concept Development	Objective Tests, Rating Scales, Checklists
Problem Solving	Multi-Choice Tests, Completion Tests, Objective Tests, Observations
Performance	Performance Tests, Objective Tests
Classroom Behavior	Anecdotal Records, Observations, Interviews, Essay Tests
Interests	Questionnaires, Surveys, Interest Inventories, Essays
Attitude	Rating Scales, Checklists, Objective Tests, Essay Tests
Social Adjustment	Rating Scales, Anecdotal Records, Interviews
Self Concern	Sociograms, Interest Inventories, Questionnaires, Essay Tests

Various types of informal techniques may be used to evaluate behaviors in several areas of learning. Rating scales, checklists, questionnaires, anecdotal reports, and objective tests may be used to evaluate behaviors. The above list is not complete, and teachers should be free to use other techniques, depending upon the abilities and disabilities of their students. Chapters 3 and 11 provide detailed information on the use of these techniques.

Bibliography

Airasian, P. W. 1994. *Classroom assessment,* 2nd ed. New York: McGraw-Hill.
——. 2000. *Assessment in the classroom: A concise approach.* New York: McGraw-Hill.
——. 2001. *Classroom assessment: Concepts and applications.* New York: McGraw-Hill.
Andrade, H. G. 2000. Using rubrics to promote thinking and learning: *Educational Leadership* 57 (5), 13–18.
Arends, R. I. 2000. *Learning to teach.* New York: McGraw-Hill.
Arter, J. 1999. Teaching about performance assessment. *Educational Measurement: Issues and Practice* 18 (2), 30–44.
Austin, S., and R. McCann. 1992. Here's another arbitary grade for your collection: A statewide study of grading policies. Paper presented at the annual meeting of the American Educational Resource Association. San Francisco: ERIC Document Reproduction Service No. 343944.
Bartz, D., S. Anderson-Robinson, and L. Hillman. 1994. Performance assessment: Make them show what they know. *Principal* 73, 11–14.
Baruth, L. G., and M. L. Manning. 1992. *Multicultural education of children and adolescents.* Boston: Allyn and Bacon.
Beaty, J. 1994. *Observing development of the young child,* 3rd ed. New York: Macmillan.
Berdine, W. H., and S. A. Meyer. 1987. *In special education.* Boston: Little, Brown and Company.
Blaisdell, E. A. 1993. *Statistics in practice.* New York: Sanders College Publishing.
Bloom, B. S., ed. 1956. Taxonomy of educational objectives. *Handbook 1: Cognitive Domain.* New York: David McKay.
Bogdan, R. C., and S. K. Biklen. 1982. *Qualitative research for education: An introduction to theory and methods.* Boston: Allyn and Bacon.

Browder, D. M. 1991. *Assessment of individuals with severe disabilities: An applied behavior approach to life skills assessment,* 2nd ed. Baltimore, Md.: Brookes.

Bruning, J. L., and B. L. Kintz. 1987. *Computational handbook of statistics,* 3rd ed. Glenview, Ill.: Scott Foresman.

Calfee, R. C. 1994. *Implications for cognitive psychology for authentic assessment and instructions* (Tech. Report No. 69). Berkeley: National Center for the Study of Writing, University of California.

Calfee, R. C., and E. H. Heibert. 1991. Classroom assessment of reading. In R. Barr, M. Kamil, P. Mosenthal., and P. D. Pearson, eds., *Handbook of research reading,* 2nd ed. New York: Longman.

Campbell, D. T., and J. C. Stanley. 1963. *Experimental and quasi-experimental design for research.* Chicago: Rand McNally.

Cannell, J. J. 1989. *How public education cheats on standardized achievement tests.* Albuquerque, N.M.: Friends of Education.

Canner, J. 1991. Regaining trust: Enhancing the credibility of school testing programs. Xerox. National Council on Measurement in Education Task Force.

Canner, J., T. Fisher, J. Fremer, T. Haladyna, J. Hall, W. Mehrens, C. Pearlman, E. Roeber, and P. Sandifer. 1991. *Regaining trust: Enhancing the credibility of school programs.* Xerox. National Council of Measurement in Education Task Force.

Carr, J. F., and D. E. Harris, 2001. *Succeeding with standards.* Alexandria, Va.: Association for Supervision and Curriculum Development.

Choate, J., B. Enright, L. Miller, J. Poteet, and R. Rakes. 1995. *Curriculum assessment and programming,* 3rd ed. Boston: Allyn and Bacon.

Cizek, G. J. 1999. *Cheating on tests: How to do it, detect it, and prevent it.* Mahwah, N.J.: Lawrence Erlbaum.

Cohen, L. G., and L. J. Spenciner. 1998. *Assessment of children and youth.* New York: Addison-Wesley Longman.

College Board. 1998. *High school grading policies.* Research notes: RN-02. Office of Research and Development. Princeton, N.J. College Boards.

Cook, T. D., and D. T. Campbell. 1979. *Quasi-experimentation.* Chicago: Rand-McNally.

Cross, L. H., and R. B. Frary. 1999. Hodge podge grading: Endorsed by students and teachers alike. *Applied Measurement in Education* 12 (1), 53–72.

Davison, D. M., and D. L. Pearce. 1992. The influence of writing activities on the mathematics learning of Native American students. *The Journal of Educational Issues of Language Minority Students* 10, 146–57.

Delpit, L. 1995. *Other people's children: Cultural conflict in the classroom.* New York: The New Press.

Dowdy, S., and S. Wearden. 1991. *Statistics for research,* 2nd ed. New York: John Wiley and Sons.

Doyle, W. 1992. Curriculum and pedagogy. In P. W. Jackson, ed., *Handbook of research in curriculum* (pp. 465–85). New York: Macmillan.

Durm, M. W. 1993. ANA is not an A is not a A: A history of grading. *The Educational Forum* 57, 294–97.

Ebel, R. L. 1970. The case for true-false test items. *School Review* 78, 373–89.

Elliott, J., J. Ysseldyke, M. Thurlow, and R. Erickson. 1998. What about assessment and accountability? Practical implications for educators. *Teaching Exceptional Children* 31 (1), 20–27.

Elmore, P. B., and P. L. Woehlke. 1997. *Basic statistics.* New York: Longman.

Fager, J. J., B. S. Blake, and J. C. Impara. 1997. Examining teacher educators' knowledge of classroom assessment: A pilot study. Paper presented at the National Council on Measurement in Education National Conference, Chicago.

Federal Register. 1977. 42 (163), 42474-42518. Washington, D.C.: U.S. Government Printing Office.

Goldring, E. B., and C. Hausman. 1997. Empower parents for productive partnership. *Education Digest* 62, 25–29.

Goodrich, H. 1997. Understanding rubrics. *Educational Leadership* 4 (4), 14–17.

Goodson, I. 1992. *Studying teacher's lives: Problems and possibilities.* New York: Teachers College Press.

Gravetter, F. J., and L. B. Wallnau. 1996. *Statistics for the behavioral sciences.* New York: West Publishing Company.

Green, R. 1998. A parent's perspective. *Exceptional Parents* 28 (8), 30–32.

Gronlund, N. E. 1991. *Constructing achievement tests,* 3rd ed. Englewood Cliffs, N.J.: Prentice-Hall.

———. 1998. *Assessment of student achievement,* 6th ed. Boston: Allyn and Bacon.

Gronlund, N. E., and R. L. Linn. 1990. *Measurement and evaluation in teaching.* New York: Macmillan.

Guild, P. 1994. The cultural learning style connection. *Educational Leadership* 51, 16–21.

Guskey, T. R. 1996. Reporting on student learning: Lessons from the past— prescriptions for the future. In T. R. Guskey, ed., *Communicating student learning* (1996 ASCD Yearbook, pp. 13–24). Alexandria, Va.: Association for Supervision and Curriculum Development.

Haladya, T. M. 1992. The effectiveness of several multiple-choice formats. *Applied Measurement and Education* 5, 73–88.

———. 1997. *Writing test items to evaluate higher order thinking.* Boston: Allyn and Bacon.

Hawkins, D. 1973. I, thou, it: The triangular relationship. In C. Silberman, ed., *The open classroom reader*. New York: Random House.

Herbert, E. A. 1992. Portfolios invite reflection from both students and staff. *Educational Leadership* 49 (8), 58–61.

Hilliard, A. G. 1989. Teachers and culture styles in a pluralistic society. *NEA Today* 7, 65–69.

Hinkle, D. E., W. Wiersma, and S. G. Jurs. 1994. *Applied statistics for the behavioral sciences*. Boston: Houghton-Mifflin Company.

Hoy, C., and N. Gregg. 1994. *Assessment: The special educator's role*. Pacific Grove, Calif.: Brooks/Cole.

Jacob, E. 1987. Qualitative research traditions: A review. *Review of Educational Research* 57, 1–50.

James, A. B. 1996. Helping the parents of a special needs child. *Lutheran Education* 132, 78–87.

Joint Advisory Committee. 1993. *Principle for fair student assessment practices for education in Canada*. Edmonton, Canada: University of Alberta.

Joint Committee on Testing Practices. 1988. *Code for fair testing practices in education*. Washington, D.C.: American Psychological Association.

Kearns, J. F., H. L. Kleinert, and G. Kennedy. 1999. We need not exclude anyone. *Educational Leadership* 56 (6), 32–38.

Kleinsassar, A. 1991. Rethinking assessment: Who's the expert? Paper presented at the Casper Outcomes Conference. Casper, Wyo.

Madaus, G. F., and L. M. O'Dwyer. 1999. A short history of performance assessment: Lessons learned. *Phi Delta Kappan* 80 (9), 688–95.

Marso, R. N., and F. L. Pigge. 1989. Elementary classroom teachers' testing needs and proficiencies: Multiple assessment and in-service training priorities. *Educational Review* 13, 1–17.

Maryland State Department of Education. 1973. *Assessing learning styles of exceptional individuals*. Baltimore, Md.: Division of Instructional Television.

Marzano, R. J. 2000. *Transforming classroom grading*. Alexandria, Va.: Association for Supervision and Curriculum Development.

Marzano, R. J., D. J. Pickering, and J. McTighe. 1993. *Assessing student outcomes: Performance assessment using the dimension of learning model*. Alexandria, Va.: Association for Supervision and Curriculum Development.

Mason, E., and A. L. Egel. 1995. What does Amy like?: Using a mini-reinforcer in instructional activities. *Teaching Exceptional Children* 28, 42–45.

McKinley, J. 1999. Observational assessment: Validating what teachers see in the classroom. *Education Update* 41, 5–6.

McLoughlin, J., and R. Lewis. 1991. *Assessing special students: Strategies and procedures,* 3rd ed. Columbus, Ohio: Charles E. Merrill.

McTighe, J. 1996. Performance-based assessment in the classroom: A planning framework. In R. Blum and J. Arter, eds. *Student performance in an era of restructuring.* Alexandria, Va.: Association for Supervision and Curriculum Development.

Mehrens, W. A., W. J. Popham, and J. M. Ryan.1998. How to prepare students for performance assessments. *Educational Measurement: Issues and Practices* 17 (1), 18–22.

Meyer, C. A. 1992. What's the difference between authentic and performance assessment? *Educational Leadership* 49, 39–40.

Meyer, L., J. Eichinger, and J. Downing. 1992. *The program quality indicators (PqI): A checklist of most promising practices in educational programs for students with severe disabilities* (rev. ed.). Syracuse, N.Y.: Syracuse University Division of Special Education and Rehabilitation.

Meyer, L., and R. Janney. 1989. User-friendly measures of meaningful outcomes: Evaluating the behavioral interventions. *Journal of the Association for Persons with Severe Handicaps* 14 (4), 263–70.

Mitchell, R. 1992. *Testing for learning.* New York: The Free Press.

O'Brien, L. 1989. Learning styles: Make the student aware. *NASSP Bulletin,* October, 85–89.

Olson, L. 1995. Cards on the table. *Education Week,* June 14, 23–28.

O'Neil, J. 1993. *The promise of portfolios.* Alexandria, Va.: Association for Supervision and Curriculum Development.

Perrone, V. 1991. *Expanding student assessment.* Alexandria, Va.: Association for Supervision and Curriculum Development.

Phillips, S. E. 1996. Legal defensibility of standards: Issues and policy perspectives. *Educational Measurement Issues and Practices* 15 (2), 5–13, 19.

Pike, K., and S. Salend. 1995. Authentic assessment strategies. *Teaching Exceptional Children* 28 (1), 15–19.

Podemski, R. C., G. E. Marsh II, T. E. Smith, and B. J. Price. 1995. *Comprehensive administration of special education,* 2nd ed. Englewood Cliffs, N.J.: Prentice-Hall.

Popham, J. W. 1991. Appropriateness of teachers' test preparation practices. *Educational Measurement: Issues and Practice* 10 (4), 12–15.

——. 2002. *Classroom assessment: What do teachers need to know?* Boston: Allyn and Bacon.

Potter, L. 1998. Making parent involvement meaningful. *Schools in the Middle* 6, 9–10.

Price, K. M., and K. L. Nelson. 1999. *Daily planning for today's classroom.* Belmont, Calif.: Wadsworth Publishing.

Putnam, M. L. 1992. Characteristics of questions on tests administered by mainstream secondary classroom teachers. *Learning Disabilities Research and Practice* 7 (3), 29–36.

Rhodes, L. K., and S. Nathension-Mejia. 1992. Anecdotal records: A powerful tool for on-going literacy assessment. *The Reading Teachers* 45 (7), 502–509.

Roth-Smith, C. 1991. *Learning disabilities: The interaction of learner, task, and setting.* Boston: Allyn and Bacon.

Ryan, J., and J. Miyasaka. 1995. Current practices in teaching and assessment: What is driving the change? *NAASP Bulletin* 79, 1–10.

Salinger, T. 1991. *Getting started with alternative assessment methods.* Workshop presented at the New York State Reading Association Conference, Lake Kiamesha, New York.

Salvia, J., and J. E. Ysseldyke. 1998. *Assessment.* Boston: Houghton-Mifflin.

Selby, D., and S. Murphy. 1992. Graded or degraded: Perceptions of letter-grading for mainstreamed learning-disabled students. *British Columbia Journal of Special Education* 16 (1), 92–104.

Shavelson, R. J., and G. P. Baxter. 1992. What we've learned about assessing hands-on science. *Educational Leadership* 49, 20–25.

Shavelson, R. J., X. Gao, and G. P. Baxter. 1992. *Sampling variability of performance assessments* (Report No. 361). Santa Barbara: University of California, National Center for Research in Evaluation, Standards, and Student Testing.

Shea, T., and A. M. Bauer. 1991. *Parents and teachers of children with disabilities: A handbook for collaboration,* 2nd ed. Boston: Allyn and Bacon.

Simon, S. B., and J. A. Bellanca, eds. 1976. *Regarding the grading myths: Primer of alternatives to grades and marks.* Alexandria, Va.: Association for Supervision and Curriculum Development.

Sperling, D. 1996. Collaborative assessment making high standards a reality for all students. In R. E. Blum and J. A. Arter, eds., *A handbook for student performance assessment in an era of restructuring.* Alexandria, Va.: Association for Supervision and Curriculum Development.

Stevenson, H. W., and J. W. Stigler. 1992. *The learning gap: Why our schools are failing and what we can learn from Japanese and Chinese education.* New York: Touchstone.

Stiggins, R. J. 1997. *Student-centered classroom assessment.* Columbus, Ohio: Prentice-Hall.

Stiggins, R. J., D. A. Frisbie, and P. A. Griswold. 1989. Inside high school grading practices: Building research agenda. Educational measurements issues and practices 8 (2), (pp. 5–14).

Stodolsky, S. S. 1989. Is teaching really by the books? In P. W. Jackson and S. Haroutunian-Gordon, eds., *Eighty-ninth yearbook of the national society for the study of education,* part I (pp. 159–84). Chicago: University of Chicago Press.

Strickland, B. B., and A. D. Turnbull. 1993. *Developing and implementing individualized education programs.* Englewood Cliffs, N.J.: Prentice-Hall.

Swanson, H. C., and B. L. Watson. 1989. *Educational and psychological assessment of exceptional children,* 2nd ed. Columbus, Ohio: Merrill Publishing.

Taylor, G. R. 1997. *Curriculum strategies: Social skills intervention for young African American males.* Westport, Conn.: Praeger.

———. 1998. *Curriculum strategies for teaching social skills to the disabled: Dealing with inappropriate behaviors.* Springfield, Ill.: Charles C. Thomas.

———. 1999. *Curriculum models and strategies for educating children with disabilities in inclusive classrooms.* Springfield, Ill.: Charles C. Thomas.

———. 2000. *Integrating quantitative and qualitative methods in research* Lanham, Md.: University Press of America.

———. 2000. *Parental involvement: A practical guide for collaboration and teamwork for students with disabilities.* Springfield, Ill.: Charles C. Thomas.

———. 2001. *Educational interventions and services for children with exceptionalities: Strategies and perspectives.* Springfield, Ill.: Charles C. Thomas.

———. 2002. *Assessing children with disabilities.* New York: Edwin Mellen Press.

Thurlow, M. L., J. L. Elliot, and J. E. Ysseldyke. 1998. *Testing students with disabilities: Practical strategies for complying with district and state requirements.* Thousand Oaks, Calif.: Corwin Press.

Turnbull, H. R. 1993. *Free appropriate public education: The law and children with disabilities,* 4th ed. Reston, Va.: Love Publishing.

Tyack, T., and W. Tobin. 1994. The "grammar" of schooling: Why has it been so hard to change? *American Educational Research Journal* 31 (3), 453–79.

Vaughn, S., J. S. Schumm, and J. B. Brick. 1998. Using a rating scale to design and evaluate inclusion programs. *Teaching Exceptional Children* 3 (4), 41–45.

Voor, R. 1997. Connecting kids and parents to school. *Education Digest* 62, 20–21.

Wallace, G., S. C. Larsen, and L. K. Elksnin. 1992. *Educational assessment of learning problems: Testing for teaching.* Boston: Allyn and Bacon.

Waterman, B. B. 1994. *Assessing children for the presence of a disability.* Washington, D.C.: National Information Center for Children and Youths with Disabilities.

Wiggins, G. 1992. Creating tests worth taking. *Educational Leadership* 49 (8), 26–33.

———. 1993a. Assessment authenticity, context, and validity. *Phi Delta Kappan*, November, 200–214.

———. 1993b. *Assessing student performance: Exploring the purpose and limits for testing.* San Francisco: Jossey-Bass.

Wiggins, G., and J. McTighe. 1998. *Understanding by design.* Alexandria, Va.: Association for Supervision and Curriculum Development.

Witt, J. C., S. N. Elliott, E. J. Daly III, F. M. Gresham, and J. J. Kramer. 1998. *Assessment of at-risk and special needs children.* New York: McGraw-Hill.

Wolf, D. P. 1989. Portfolio assessment: Sampling student work. *Educational Leadership* 46 (7), 35–39.

Wrinkle, W. L. 1947. *Improving marking and reporting practices in elementary and secondary schools.* New York: Holt, Rinehart, and Winston.

Glossary

Anecdotal Record—A short written report of an individual's behavior in a specific situation or circumstance.

Assessment—The process of collecting, synthesizing, and interpreting information to aid classroom decision making, including information gathered about pupils, instruction, and classroom climate.

Assessment Accommodations—The techniques employed when assessing individuals with disabilities in order to secure more valid inferences about each student's knowledge and skills. Commonly used accommodations include allowing increased time to complete an activity and presenting the testing format in a style familiar to the student.

Checklist—A written list of performance criteria associated with a special activity in which an observer marks the pupil's performance on each criterion.

Educational Objectives—Statements that describe a pupil's accomplishment that will result from instruction; the statement describes the behavior the pupil will learn to perform and the content on which it will be performed.

Essay Item—A test item requiring a response of one or more paragraphs.

Evaluation—Judging quality or goodness of a performance or a course of action.

Grade—A symbol used by a teacher to represent a pupil's achievement in a content area.

Instructional Assessment—Collection, synthesis, and interpretation of information needed to make decisions about planning or carrying out instruction.

Instructional Objectives—Specific objectives used to plan and conduct instruction.

Item Alternatives—The answer options used in a multiple-choice test item.

Mean—The arithmetic average of a set of scores.

Median—The midpoint in a set of scores when the scores are ranked from lowest to highest.

Multiple-Choice Test Item—A test item requiring students to choose a response from three or more presented options.

Observation—Watching and recording a pupil's performance on an activity or project.

Performance Assessment—Observing and judging a pupil's demonstrated skill in performing an activity.

Performance Criteria—The aspects of a performance or product that are observed and assessed.

Portfolio—A well-defined assessment of pupil's performances that shows achievement of skills.

Preassessment—A pretest given before instruction to determine entry skills and knowledge, and used as part of a pretest/post-test collection of evidence regarding the quality of instruction.

Rating Scale—A written list of performance criteria related to a special activity in which an observer marks the pupil's performance on each criterion in terms of its quality.

Rubric—A scoring guide that describes varied levels of quality of student performance or product assessment.

Scoring Rubric—A rating scale based upon written descriptions of varied levels of achievement in a performance assessment.

Self-Assessment—Making a pupil responsible for judging and critiquing his or her performance or product according to clear performance criteria.

Short-Answer Item—A test item eliciting a brief response from students.

Teaching to the Test—When a teacher directs instruction toward the assessment domain represented by the test or toward specific items that make up the actual test.

True-False Item—A common binary-choice item in which the student's two options regarding the accuracy of a presented statement are *true* or *false*.

Author Index

Airasian, P. W., 11, 12, 21, 22, 31, 33, 35, 39, 41–43, 48, 50, 58, 108
Anderson-Robinson, S., 40
Andrade, H. G., 50
Arends, R. I., 1
Arter, J., 42
Austin, S., 109

Bartz, D. S., 49
Baruth, L. G., 68
Bauer, A. M., 85, 112
Beaty, J., 47
Bellanca, J. A., 109
Berdine, W. H., 115
Biklen, S. K., 77
Blaisdell, E. A., 77
Blake, B. S., 42
Bloom, B. S., 2
Bogdan, R. C., 77
Brick, J. B., 48
Browder, D. M., 19
Bruning, J., L., 77

Calfee, R. C., 15
Campell, D. T., 78
Cannell, J. J., 35
Canner, J., 31, 32, 34

Carr, J. F., 3
Choate, J. B., 100
Cizek, G. J., 35
Cohen, L. G., 47, 123
College Board, 109
Cook, D. T., 78
Cross, L. H., 107

Daly, E. J., 19, 45
Davison, D. M., 49
Delpit, L. 4
Dowdy, S., 72, 77
Doyle, W., 108
Durm, M. W., 26

Ebel, R. L., 22
Egel, A. L., 51, 59
Elksnin, L. K., 12, 15
Elliott, S. N., 19, 29, 45, 116
Enright, B., 100
Erickson, R., 29, 45

Fager, J. J., 42
Federal Register, 84, 85
Fisher, T., 34
Fray, R. B., 107
Frisbie, D. A., 109

Subject Index